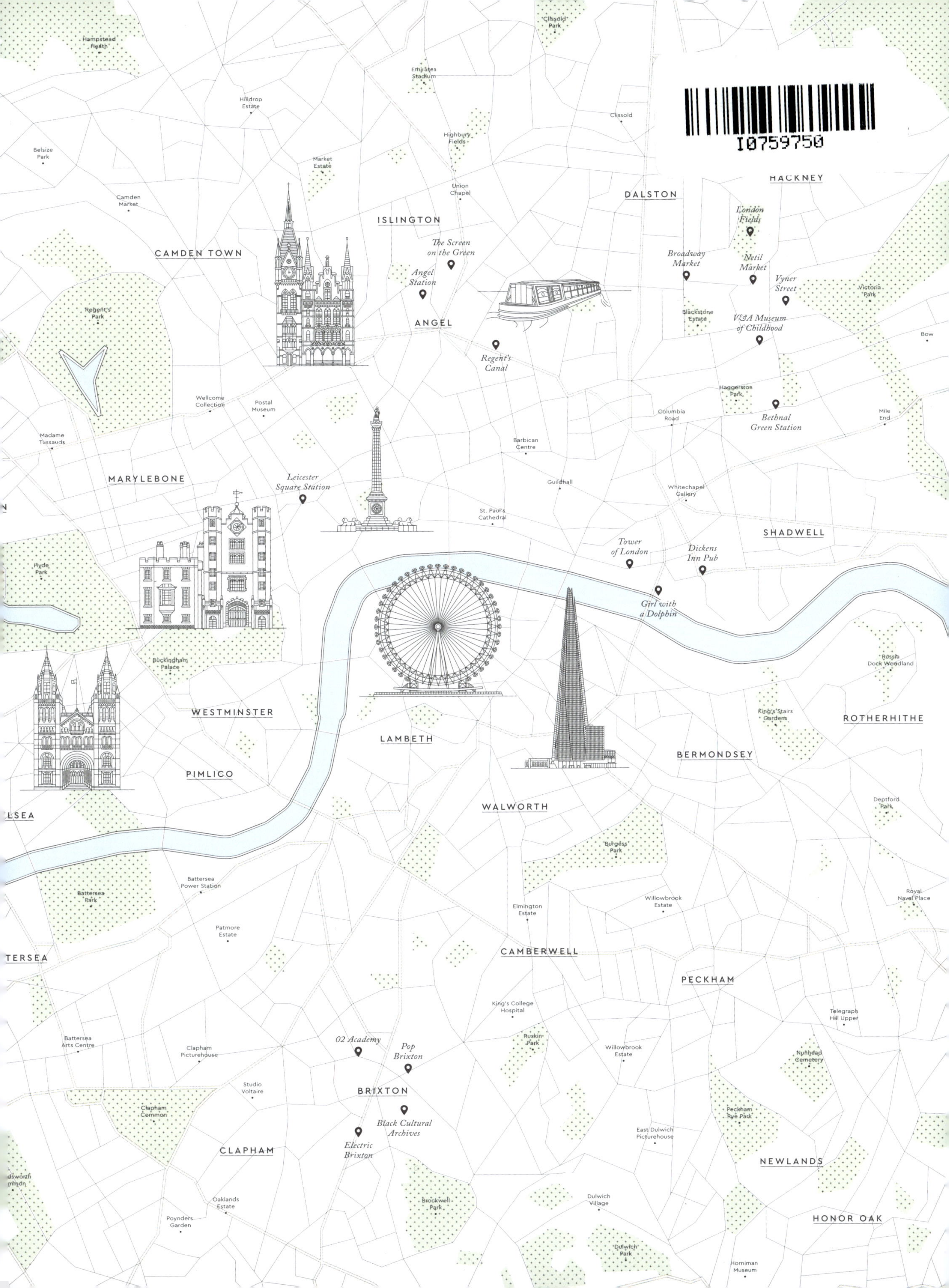
Hampstead Heath
Clissold Park
Emirates Stadium
Hilldrop Estate
Clissold
Highbury Fields
Belsize Park
Market Estate
Union Chapel
Camden Market
HACKNEY
DALSTON
ISLINGTON
London Fields
CAMDEN TOWN
The Screen on the Green
Broadway Market
Netil Market
Angel Station
Vyner Street
Victoria Park
Regent's Park
Blackstone Estate
V&A Museum of Childhood
ANGEL
Bow
Regent's Canal
Haggerston Park
Wellcome Collection
Postal Museum
Columbia Road
Bethnal Green Station
Mile End
Madame Tussauds
Barbican Centre
MARYLEBONE
Leicester Square Station
Guildhall
Whitechapel Gallery
St. Paul's Cathedral
SHADWELL
Tower of London
Dickens Inn Pub
Hyde Park
Girl with a Dolphin
Buckingham Palace
Russia Dock Woodland
WESTMINSTER
King's Stairs Gardens
ROTHERHITHE
LAMBETH
BERMONDSEY
PIMLICO
WALWORTH
Deptford Park
Burgess Park
Battersea Power Station
Battersea Park
Royal Naval Place
Willowbrook Estate
Elmington Estate
Patmore Estate
CAMBERWELL
PECKHAM
King's College Hospital
Telegraph Hill Upper
Battersea Arts Centre
O2 Academy
Pop Brixton
Clapham Picturehouse
Ruskin Park
Willowbrook Estate
Nunhead Cemetery
Studio Voltaire
BRIXTON
Clapham Common
Black Cultural Archives
Peckham Rye Park
East Dulwich Picturehouse
Electric Brixton
CLAPHAM
NEWLANDS
Oaklands Estate
Dulwich Village
Brockwell Park
Poynders Garden
HONOR OAK
Dulwich Park
Horniman Museum

LONDON

LONDON

VALENTINE BENOIST | LAURA JALBERT

INTRODUCTION

The 18th-century intellectual Samuel Johnson said that "when a man is tired of London, he is tired of life", a sentiment that still holds true today. London is a vibrant city and a unique playground for explorers in search of pleasure and adventure.

London has demonstrated its resilience repeatedly throughout the trials and tribulations it has faced. Having been ravaged by the Great Fire of 1666, it was rebuilt under the guidance of architect Christopher Wren and, after weathering the destruction of the Blitz in World War II, it has reinvented itself to be a modern city. In what is a historical melting pot, the last vestiges of the Middle Ages, futuristic skyscrapers, grandiose Georgian townhouses, renovated warehouses, (almost) period Victorian pubs, and shiny rooftops all stand alongside quite happily.

The Romans founded *Londinium* on the site of the current City of London in the 1st century, and the settlement was later to be shaped and expanded by the Saxons and Normans in succession. London has been a commercial center since the Middle Ages and saw its economic fortunes prosper under the Tudors (1485-1603) thanks to an upswing in maritime trade. The city is still a major international commercial, political, and cultural hub.

These successive waves of expansion eventually resulted in Greater London, which now extends over 607 square miles (1,572 km^2) and is fifteen times the size of Paris! With over 9 million inhabitants, it is one of the most populous cities in Europe, although the population density is actually quite low and its thirty-two boroughs (administrative districts) often have a distinctly village-like feel. You may well feel that you are in the middle of the countryside as you roam Hampstead Heath, that you are mastering the British sense of style in the mews of Mayfair, or diving back into the era of the Industrial Revolution in Hackney. The actual City of London is an entity in itself.

This diversity is mainly cultural, however, and with more than three hundred languages spoken, the city's cosmopolitan nature still adds spice to the mixture, despite Brexit. From the underground scene to its avant-garde galleries, from Camden to Notting Hill via Brixton, it is a cultural hub enriched by inhabitants drawn from every corner of the globe. Despite being a magnet for lovers of art, music, architecture, fashion design, and gourmet food, London can demonstrate a somewhat British reserve at times, but its eclecticism and dynamism are unmissable. Last, but by no means least, you can be in nature everywhere: the widest boundaries of Greater London contain 3,000 parks and gardens covering 47 percent of its surface area, providing easily accessible green escapes that offer a welcome alternative to the hustle and bustle of the capital.

Deptford Bridge
453
LTZ 1879

BLOOMSBURY, CHINATOWN, CLERKENWELL, CITY, COVENT GARDEN, HOLBORN, SOHO

CENTRAL EAST

From the literary history of Bloomsbury to the City skyscrapers, taking in Covent Garden's theaters, steamy nights in Soho and Clerkenwell's design scene, the areas east of Regent Street are in the thick of the action in London.

P.8

The listed building of All Souls, just north of Regent Street, is often used for broadcasts by the neighboring BBC.

OPPOSITE

This single-minded thrift store only sells vintage Burberry clothing and accessories. Very British!

The "City" on the northeastern bank of the Thames is the historic and financial center of London. It is also known as the Square Mile because of its area (which equates to 2.9 km^2) and this postage stamp with the influence of a capital city is in fact an independent entity. Managed by the City of London Corporation, it even has its own Lord Mayor. Now a maze of skyscrapers and financial institutions, the City was where the Romans laid the first stones of Londinium, although its international and cosmopolitan energy fades completely as soon as evening comes.

The London Museum to the northwest of the City charts the trajectory from Roman settlement to contemporary metropolis, and you can still see traces of the route of the London Wall, the fortification surrounding the ancient Roman city, running between the Tower of London and the Barbican, a Brutalist icon on the outskirts of Clerkenwell.

Smithfield Market, a historic meat market that remained in operation until 2023, was also located on the edge of a district once dominated by watchmakers and printers, and the London Museum is set to move into the metal structure of this Victorian edifice, so iconic of the area, in 2026. Clerkenwell is in the throes of reinventing itself but also boasts former warehouses, design showrooms, and unmissable restaurants, such as those around Exmouth Market.

With its relentless crowds, neon lights, and endless ballet of double-decker buses and black cabs, this is the very epicenter of the cultural, commercial, and tourist metropolis, and there is a real buzz of activity in this eastern part of the West End that reaches all the way to Piccadilly Circus. Soho's nightlife never sleeps amid the constant succession of plays and musicals in so-called Theatreland, around Covent Garden.

Adjacent to the frenetic center, Holborn and Bloomsbury are administratively part of the borough of Camden. The former has a legal and historical bent while the latter is the beating heart of intellectual and academic London. The eponymous Bloomsbury Group made the area its London headquarters at the turn of the 20th century and the social and aesthetic principles of this progressive circle of British writers, intellectuals, philosophers, and artists (including the likes of Virginia Woolf and John Maynard Keynes) left a lasting mark on the country's culture. The area's leafy streets, elegant facades, and Georgian squares (such as Russell Square) make it a haven of tranquility a mere a stone's throw from the hustle and bustle.

CHECK IT

CENTRAL EAST

THE ESSENTIALS

01

BRITISH MUSEUM

The most popular tourist site in the country, with exhibits that include cultural treasures such as the Rosetta Stone.

02

BLOOMSBURY SQUARE

An oasis of greenery in the heart of Bloomsbury, this garden is surrounded by magnificent Victorian terraces that were once home to celebrities such as Gertrude Stein and Benjamin Disraeli.

03

COVENT GARDEN

The pedestrianized piazza of Covent Garden in the West End is home to stores and restaurants much frequented by tourists.

04

LONDON WALL

This defensive wall constructed by the Romans around 200 BCE once surrounded the town of Londinium, and some traces still remain to this day.

05

OXFORD STREET

This famous road in the heart of London is a mecca for shoppers, with more than 300 stores along its mile and a half (2.4 km) length.

06

LEICESTER SQUARE

Statues of Shakespeare, Paddington Bear, and Laurel and Hardy look down on the tourists that flock to this famous square in the West End.

07

LIBERTY

This iconic department store was founded in 1924 and is spread over three atriums. Its architecture and its fabric prints are world-famous.

08

ROYAL OPERA HOUSE

Floating above Floral Street, the award-winning Bridge of Aspiration designed by WilkinsonEyre links the Royal Opera House and the Royal Ballet School.

09

NATIONAL GALLERY

The National Gallery in Trafalgar Square opened its doors in 1824, and its collections showcase European painting from the 13th century to the 1900s.

10

SOHO

This district is a hive of cultural, festive, musical, and gastronomic activity that sees Londoners and visitors mingling at all hours of the day and night.

11

FORTNUM & MASON

Fortnum's have specialized in tea to delight the palates of London high society since 1707, and the Food Halls are a must-visit.

12

TRAFALGAR SQUARE

This famous square was named to commemorate the British victory over the empire of Napoleon I at the Battle of Trafalgar in 1805.

Smithf
Tap

ABOVE

Charming Neal's Yard is a gem nestling in the heart of Seven Dials that is often missed by visitors.

OPPOSITE

Charterhouse Street in Farringdon is best known for Fabric, a legendary London nightclub.

ARCHITECTURE

BARBICAN

A BRUTALIST ICON

A city within a city, this icon of post-war Brutalist architecture is a hybrid entity within which daily life and artistic institutions coexist in harmony.

The London of the 1950s had been badly damaged by bombing and needed to be reimagined. The project by architects Chamberlin, Powell and Bon produced a mixed space combining homes, culture, and the natural world that breathed radical new life into 40 acres (16 ha) of this old textile district within the City that had been destroyed in the Blitz.

Building on the foundations of Londinium, some of which were cunningly incorporated into the architecture, the architects of the Barbican Estate hoped to attract "young professionals who enjoy Mediterranean vacations, French cuisine, and Scandinavian design" into a then-deserted Square Mile. Their ambitious plan was rounded off with bars and restaurants, an esplanade, hanging gardens, pubs, and an exceptional artistic and cultural hub called the Barbican Centre. Work began in 1965 and the area was opened by Queen Elizabeth II in 1982, some twenty years and 130,000 cubic meters of concrete later.

Since then, the audacious concrete island, an icon of Brutalist architecture, has seemed to hover above the vehicle traffic thanks to its ingenious system of highwalks (footbridges popular with 1960s town planners). From its artificial lake constructed above the Circle Line to the cinema dug 15 feet (5 m) below sea level, every detail of this complex project has been meticulously thought through, and its famous towers (named Shakespeare, Cromwell, and Lauderdale respectively) are now an integral part of the London skyline!

The Barbican has been a listed building since 2001 and is home to more than 4,000 residents sympathetic to its aesthetics. The best ways to appreciate the building include exploring the secrets of its labyrinths on a guided architectural tour, lingering in the esplanade café, immersing yourself in the library's collection of artistic and musical works, or perhaps taking a stroll through the astonishing winter garden. Nothing beats the Barbican Conservatory for a special Sunday treat! This spectacular greenhouse was built to hide the theater's mechanical apparatus from the view of Cromwell Tower residents and it seems to float between the apartments and the arts center. It is the green lung of this concrete jungle and home to more than 1,800 plant species from around the world, along with fish and freshwater turtles.

The Barbican Centre is the largest performing arts hub in Europe and has rapidly established itself as a venue of international importance. The concert hall is the permanent home of the London Symphony Orchestra (LSO) and the center also plays host to performances by the Royal Shakespeare Company (RSC), experimental productions, cinema screenings, and contemporary art exhibitions that regularly garner praise from critics. It has become a pillar of London's cultural scene.

STYLISH HOMES

The complex's twenty buildings house some 2,000 apartments that are much sought after amongst aesthetes.

URBAN JUNGLE

Nestling amongst the concrete, the vegetation of the Barbican Conservatory provides a haven of greenery that is unique in London.

ABBOTT and HOLDER
30a
29
29
PAUL STOLPER
Tara

ABOVE

Tucked away behind the arcades of one of its entrances on Piccadilly, the Royal Academy of Arts has been promoting the visual arts since 1768.

OPPOSITE

The art galleries of Museum Street rub shoulders with cafés and bookshops in Bloomsbury.

Tiny lanes like Long's Court, just around the corner from Leicester Square, show a different side of the center of the capital.

Tower Hill tube station with its historic tiling is located on the District and Circle Lines, close to historic sites like the Tower of London.

LIFESTYLE

THE NED LONDON

MILLIE'S LOUNGE

The restaurant in the large main hall serves classics of British cuisine from dawn until late into the night.

NEW LIFE

Nick Jones, the founder of Soho House & Co, has breathed new life into this building designed in the heart of the City by Sir Edwin "Ned" Lutyens in 1924.

WELLNESS

The treatment areas occupying three floors of this historic building are reserved for members and include everything you could wish for: a nail salon, spa, physiotherapists, hairdresser/barbershop, and gym.

A UNIQUE BAR

With its retractable roof, the rooftop members' bar has a spectacular view of St. Paul's.

THE FOOD HALL

Tables can be reserved at the ten establishments in this micro-city, offering specialties from around the world.

AN EXCLUSIVE ROOFTOP

Designed by Soho House, a heated pool overlooking the city awaits guests.

GLAMOROUS ROOMS

The decoration of the 250 hotel rooms incorporates elements of 1920s aesthetics.

AN UNUSUAL SETTING

In the former headquarters of the Midland Bank, bank officials have passed on the torch to the elegant barmen employed at the Ned, a luxury hotel and private club.

QUEEN ELIZABE

ABOVE

The Neoclassical facade of the British Museum features a portico of eight Doric columns and a triangular pediment decorated with sculptures.

OPPOSIE

The spiral staircase surrounding the British Museum Reading Room in the Queen Elizabeth II Great Court is the work of architect Norman Foster and was completed in 2000.

FOOD AND DRINK

ST. JOHN

THE ORIGINS OF MODERN BRITISH FOOD

In the beginning of modern British food was St. John, and the thirty-year-old flagship of the six London establishments (with an associated vineyard in Minervois) run by chef Fergus Henderson and restaurateur Trevor Gulliver is showing no signs of age.

What is the secret of their longevity? "Cooking requires consistency, a far cry from trends that come and go", as Fergus is wont to repeat. This precise vision, spurning fashions, applies equally to the setting, with its refined decor, impeccable uniforms, spotless napery, minimalist crockery, and balloon glasses. A simplicity rooted in common sense has held sway at St. John since the outset as they bring a modern twist to neglected British classics. The menu is dictated by local and seasonal produce, laying the foundations for cooking that is contemporary and British and "the only way forward", according to the chef.

Fergus gave up his architecture degree for the stove at the turn of the 1990s and, with his wife Margot (chef at Rochelle Canteen), made a name for himself upstairs at the legendary French House in Soho. Restaurateur Trevor Gulliver earned his stripes at the Fire Station in Waterloo, which featured the capital's first open kitchen.

Their first meeting, through an olive oil supplier, marked the beginning of a legend, and the pair took over an old, abandoned smokehouse from the Georgian era just round the corner from the halls of Smithfield meat market. The partners opened their restaurant at 26 St. John Street in 1995 and it quickly became a fixture on London's culinary scene.

Fast-forward thirty years and their establishment's reputation has spread internationally, largely thanks to their famous "nose to tail" approach that is celebrated on their plates daily. The principle behind it is a holistic understanding of cooking that appreciates every part of an animal, as summed up by the pig icon that features in the restaurant's logo; the foundation of the revival of English cuisine.

Ears, offal, tongues, and feet. Not a morsel goes to waste! House classics include the renowned roast bone marrow and parsley salad, decadent beef mince on dripping toast, devilled kidneys on toast, and grilled lamb's heart with radicchio and anchovy. Behind all these rather austere titles lurk dishes full of vibrancy and flavor, a nourishing cuisine with no pretension but great precision. The menu, which changes twice a day, also contains sweet indulgences such as the classic dozen madeleines, cooked to order and served still steaming, or a typical Eton mess made with raspberries. This is an essential establishment that continues to inspire whole generations of chefs.

OPEN ALL HOURS

The chilled bar space is open for a coffee, lunch or supper from morning to evening.

BRITISH CLASSICS

All the classics in the British culinary repertoire are celebrated at St. John.

ABOVE

English shoemakers compete in elegance and refinement along St. James's.

OPPOSITE

Black cabs and double-decker buses process down the famous curves of Regent Street near Piccadilly Circus.

139
TAXI
KE21 LGX
20

12
19

ABOVE

As you leave St. Dunstan in the East Church Garden, you will catch a glimpse of the Shard.

OPPOSITE

Founded in 675, All Hallows by the Tower is the oldest church in the City and can be seen from the arcades of the Tower Hill Memorial.

DEEP DIVE

SKYSCRAPERS

First appearing on the skyline in the 1980s, skyscrapers have since become a key feature of the landscape of urban London.

The dawn of the 21st century saw the United Kingdom enjoying a period of economic prosperity driven by the City bankers, and it was keen to advertise itself as a significant financial center. Following the New York model, skyscrapers began to take over the London skyline as symbols of power and modernity.

Breaking away from London's historically horizontal architecture, towers began to shoot up along the Thames, and the 365-ft (111-m) tip of St. Paul's was surpassed in 1980 by the 600-ft (183-m) Tower 42. Designed by the architect Richard Seifert, this three-sided prism symbolized the dynamism of NatWest, the bank that commissioned the project. The building is often cited as the first true skyscraper in the City, but by 1991, it was the turn of One Canada Square, the beacon project of the new business district developed on Canary Wharf, to rise to a new record height of 770 feet (235 m).

This enthusiasm for skyscrapers continued into the 2000s under the leadership of mayor Ken Livingstone. It was an era of vertical growth, with the construction of many iconic buildings, including 30 St. Mary Axe (2003), designed by the architect Norman Foster, whose helical shape has earned it the affection nickname of The Gherkin. Nature even managed to put in an appearance in a few of these monumental building sites, such as the Uruguayan architect Rafael Viñoly's 20 Fenchurch Street (2009), The Walkie-Talkie, at the top of whose thirty-eight floors is London's highest public green space, with bars and restaurants perched at a height exceeding 510 feet (155 m). This Mediterranean oasis designed by the renowned landscape architects Gillespies enjoys wonderful views of the capital and can be accessed free of charge with a reservation.

Architects are vying in inventiveness to preserve protected views of the Tower of London and Westminster Palace, and some of the most impressive examples include 122 Leadenhall Street (2014), designed by Rogers Stirk Harbour + Partners, whose tapering profile has earned it the name The Cheesegrater, Renzo Piano's famous Shard (2012) south of the Thames, whose 1,017 feet (310 m) make it the tallest building in the country, and the keen blade of The Scalpel by Kohn Pedersen Fox, which was completed in 2018 and now houses offices.

The frenzy is now slowing in tandem with the economy but, in the purest London tradition, this spontaneous urban development continues to leave a lasting mark, making this world city a unique architectural melting pot in which historic monuments and avant-garde innovations coexist in perfect harmony.

LONDON'S SKYSCRAPERS

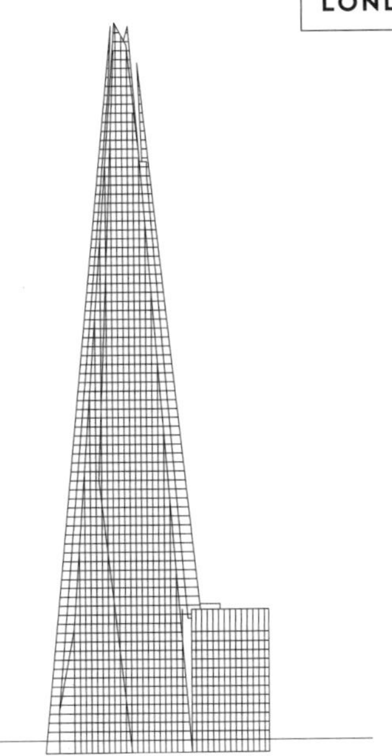

1/ THE SHARD – 1,017 FEET (310 M)

Clad in 11,000 glass panels, the building has no fewer than 44 elevators to serve its 95 floors.

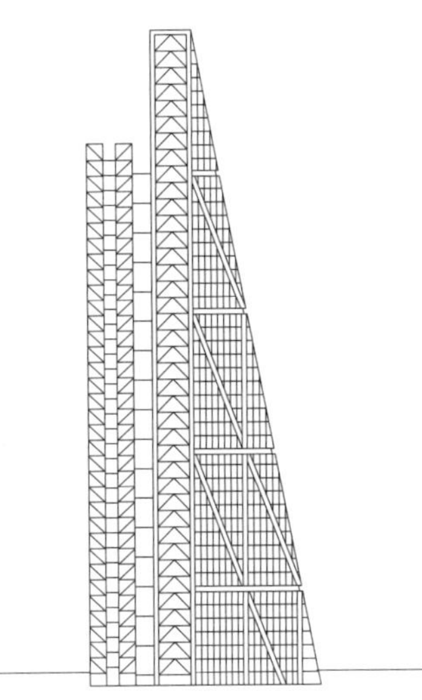

2/ THE CHEESEGRATER – 738 FEET (225 M)

To comply with strict town planning rules, each of its 45 stories is exactly 2½ feet (750 mm) narrower than the previous one.

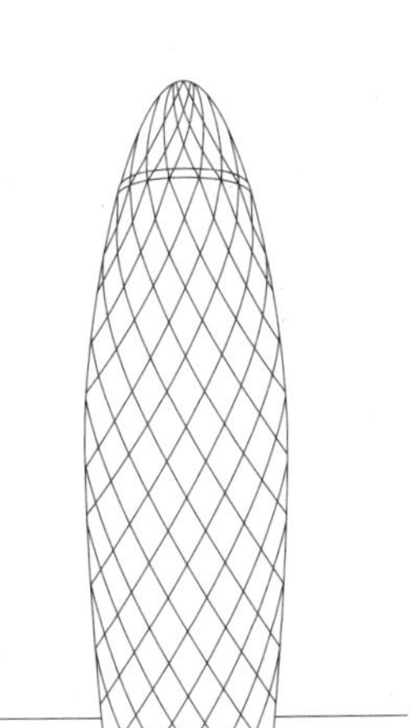

3/ THE GHERKIN – 590 FEET (180 M)

Contrary to what the shape might suggest, only the cupola at the top of the building is made of curved glass, allowing diners to enjoy a panoramic view from the restaurant and bar on the top floor.

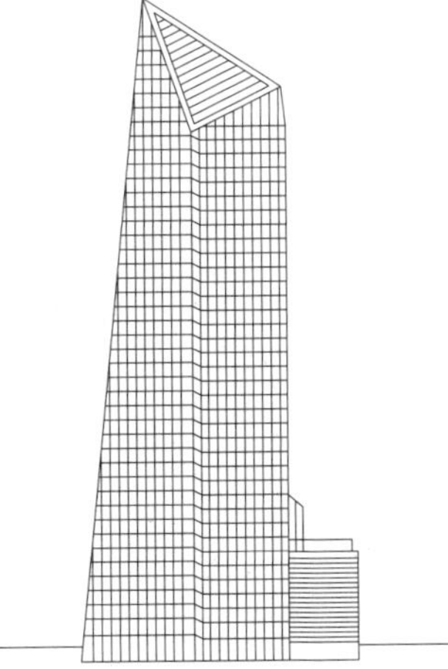

4/ THE SCALPEL – 620 FEET (190 M)

The tapering design of this 42-storey tower is not just for aesthetic effect but minimizes the effects of wind.

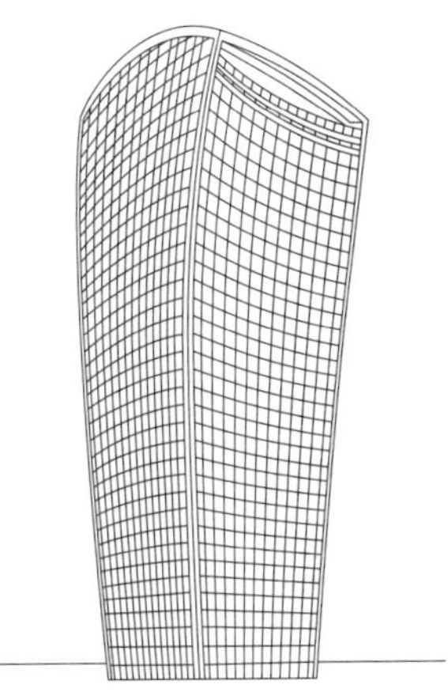

5/ THE WALKIE-TALKIE – 525 FEET (160 M)

More than 9,000 tonnes of steel went into the frame of this building, which has attracted some criticism and the name The Fryscraper for the amount of sun its south-facing glass facade reflects.

ABOVE

The windows of the Art Deco Mortimer House in Fitzrovia look out onto the BT Tower.

OPPOSITE

The view from the exit of Liverpool Street station is a perfect illustration of the architectural gallimaufry so typical of the capital.

P.36–37

The home of the Neoclassical architect John Soane (1753–1837) opposite Lincoln's Inn Fields has been turned into a museum.

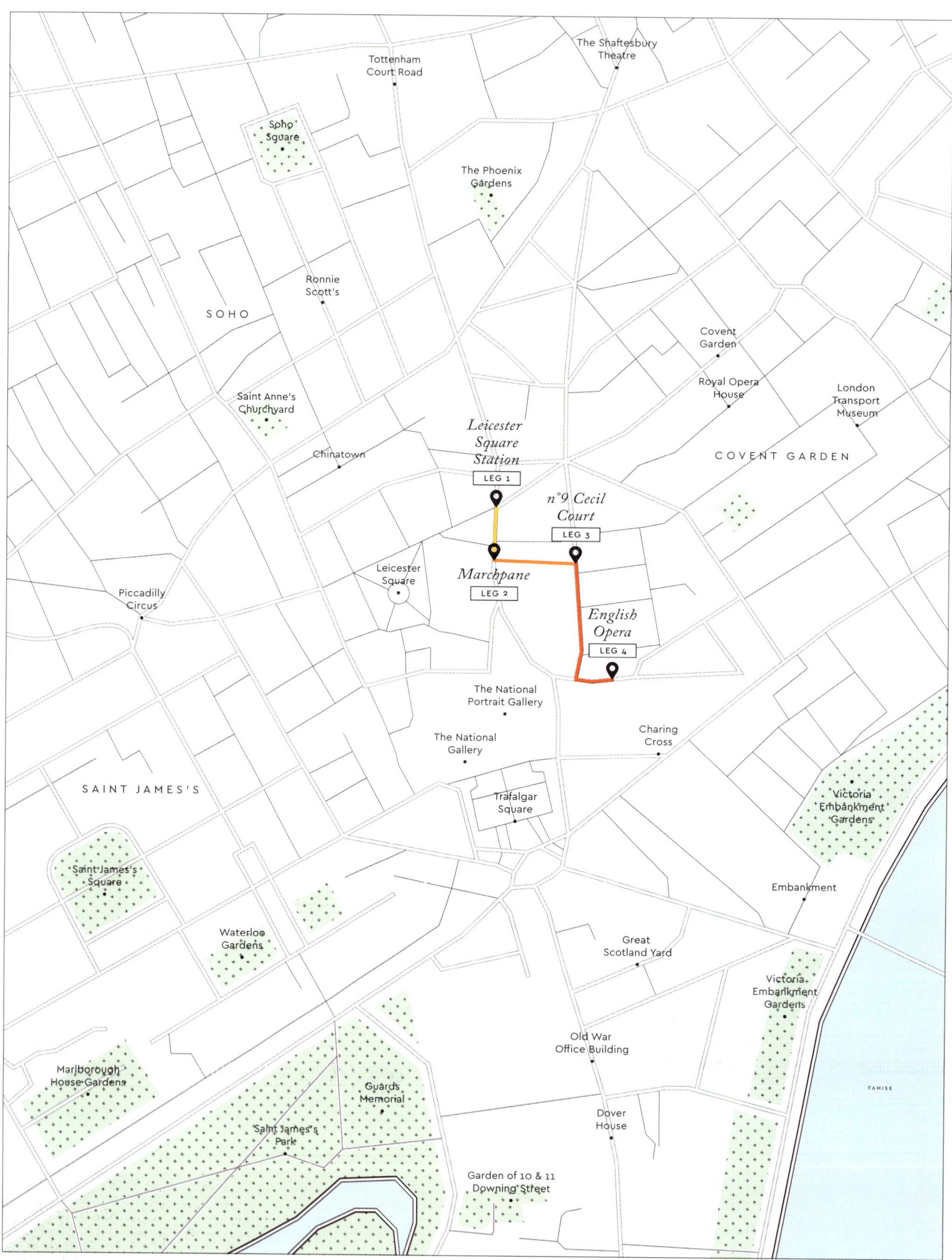

The Shaftesbury Theatre
Tottenham Court Road
Soho Square
The Phoenix Gardens
Ronnie Scott's
SOHO
Covent Garden
Royal Opera House
London Transport Museum
Saint Anne's Churchyard
Leicester Square Station
Chinatown
COVENT GARDEN
LEG 1
n°9 Cecil Court
LEG 3
Leicester Square
Marchpane
LEG 2
Piccadilly Circus
English Opera
LEG 4
The National Portrait Gallery
The National Gallery
Charing Cross
SAINT JAMES'S
Trafalgar Square
Victoria Embankment Gardens
Saint James's Square
Embankment
Waterloo Gardens
Great Scotland Yard
Victoria Embankment Gardens
Old War Office Building
Marlborough House Gardens
Guards Memorial
TAMISE
Dover House
Saint James's Park
Garden of 10 & 11 Downing Street

CECIL COURT

"Thank God! Cecil Court remains Cecil Court...", as the British author Graham Greene wrote in his autobiography *Ways of Escape*. This small lane, one of the oldest in Covent Garden, is a haven of tranquility in the heart of the West End and has witnessed many artistic endeavors in the fields of music, cinema, and literature.

LEG 1 : FLICKER ALLEY

Turn left out of Leicester Square station into the Charing Cross Road, then take the second left after St. Martin's Court to reach Cecil Court, aka Booksellers' Row. The signwriting on the shopfronts in the passage is straight out of the Victorian era and advertises some twenty dedicated and highly specialist antiquarian dealers and bookshops. Look up as you reach number 27 and you will see a green plaque commemorating the crucial role the lane played in the early years of British cinema between 1887 and 1915, to the point it was renamed Flicker Alley in a nod to the unsteady images of the first movies. A year after the first cinematograph was debuted in the United Kingdom and a decade before the very first cinema opened its doors, pioneers of the "seventh art" had settled here, along with the director Cecil Hepworth, the AHRB Centre for British Film and Television Studies and international firms such as Gaumont, Nordisk, and American Vitagraph, to name but a few. Some forty players in this new industry made this the heyday of Edwardian Cecil Court and its slightly superannuated charm still makes it a popular location for shooting historical films.

LEG 2 : MARCHPANE

Number 16 houses a typically British oddity, a bookseller specializing in rare children's books. Marchpane welcomes discerning enthusiasts in search of a first edition of *Winnie-the-Pooh* or a signed copy of *Harry Potter*. Most importantly, however, it has been an incredible collection of works by Lewis Carroll that has made the reputation of Kenneth Fuller's den since 1989. With one of the largest collections in the world of texts dedicated to *Alice's Adventures in Wonderland*, there is enough to drive you mad, but then "all the best people are", as Alice would be the first to tell you.

LEG 3 : MUSIC, MAESTRO!

There are two compulsory stops for music lovers in Cecil Court, and the first is a pilgrimage to number 9, for it was here in his barber's shop that John Couzin put up Mozart and his family in 1764 as they passed through London to give concerts. Legend has it that the child prodigy even composed his first symphony here at the age of eight. The second stop is at number 17, for the Travis & Emery Music Bookshop, a favorite haunt of London musicians. Since 1960, this bookseller with its green shopfront has stocked a selection of rare works on musicology, methods and exercises, centuries-old scores, opera libretti, and sonic treasures of all kinds and all prices. The owner, Giles Sandeman-Allen, will take every trouble to guide you through the twenty-odd thousand volumes that are regularly in stock.

LEG 4 : NOVEMBER BOOKS

Fans of alternative culture should head to the basement at number 7 (having made an appointment first, of course), where Paul Lawrence has been running November Books since 2010. This former textile designer who once worked for Vivienne Westwood has become a go-to source of publications on fashion, design, art, music and photography. Lookbooks from defunct labels, signed first editions of books of Japanese photography, complete runs of indie magazines, the thirty-something has amassed a unique collection and will be able to dig out the rare copy that has evaded you for so long. After finishing your shopping, head to the far end of the street and turn into St. Martins Lane for the English National Opera (ENO).

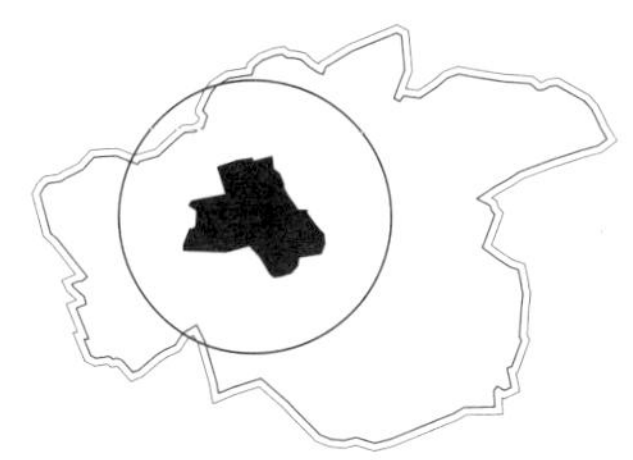

FITZROVIA, HYDE PARK, MARYLEBONE, MAYFAIR, PICCADILLY, ST. JAMES'S

CENTRAL WEST

Blending typical British elegance with a more relaxed sophistication, the historic districts of the West End (St. James's and Mayfair) join Marylebone and Fitzrovia to form the western center of the UK's capital. This is a timeless area, where homegrown British glamor rubs shoulders with chic bohemian living.

P.40

There are views of many of the city's great monuments from St. James's Park, including Buckingham Palace and the London Eye.

OPPOSITE

The fancy Georgian-style homes of Upper Grosvenor Street in Mayfair are just round the corner from Hyde Park.

The junction built at Piccadilly Circus in 1819 to link Regent Street to Piccadilly has a busy, cosmopolitan energy, as does Leicester Square. The Fortnum & Mason department store and the shopping arcades clearly show how the area has been developed for business and tourism.

As soon as you head west along Piccadilly, however, things become a little swankier. The St. James's area is steeped in history and boasts many links with the British monarchy and its royal residences. Since the 17th century, it has also been a popular haunt of the aristocracy, who frequented gentlemen's clubs and the superb St. James's Park and Green Park. Jermyn Street is renowned for its tailors, much like Savile Row in Mayfair.

Mayfair is one of the most exclusive neighborhoods in the world and its Georgian architecture and charming green spaces (such as Grosvenor Square) have long made it popular with London's high society. Some of its streets, including Bond Street and Park Lane, are very fashionable, with a host of palaces, haute couture jewelers, auction houses, and sophisticated restaurants.

Hyde Park on the western outskirts of this area is the green lung of London and, in the middle of its 350 acres (142 ha), you can rent a pedalo or take a dip in the Serpentine, or watch speechmakers harangue passers-by on Speakers's Corner near Marble Arch, a symbol of free speech since 1872.

Marylebone and Fitzrovia to the northwest are the epitome of London's village spirit. Fitzrovia has a lively and eclectic feel, with its harmonious array of different architectural eras. Once an industrial area (and still home to workshops and factories), it has since been taken over by creatives, media types, and communicators, as witnessed by Broadcasting House, the headquarters of the BBC, and the BT Tower. The area around Rathbone Place and Goodge Street is full of galleries, cafés, and antique dealers while the urban village of Marylebone is concentrated around Marylebone High Street with its tasteful boutiques and delis. The area is home to many medical professionals around Harley Street, and you will also find the Wallace Collection around the corner, along with the Chiltern Firehouse, an impressive red-brick edifice that has been converted into a luxury hotel.

CENTRAL WEST

THE ESSENTIALS

13

ALBERT MEMORIAL

This 156-ft/47.5-m monument in Kensington Gardens was commissioned by Queen Victoria in memory of her husband Albert.

14

GREEN PARK

The tree-lined paths of this royal park offer a welcome respite from busy Piccadilly, just a stone's throw away.

15

PICCADILLY CIRCUS

This square, built in 1819 to link Regent Street and Piccadilly, is famous for its giant neon signs.

16

BUCKINGHAM PALACE

Buckingham Palace has been the official residence of the British sovereign since 1837 and is surrounded by parks in the heart of London.

17

HYDE PARK

Pedalos and boats are afloat on the Serpentine, in the heart of the royal park of Hyde Park from April to October.

18

SERPENTINE

These two contemporary art galleries on Kensington Gardens are world-famous, and a renowned artist creates a temporary pavilion here every summer.

19

PICCADILLY ARCADE

This elegant Edwardian shopping mall between Piccadilly and Jermyn Street opened its doors in 1909.

20

ROYAL ARCADE

This colorful Victorian-era shopping arcade looking out over Old Bond Street opened in 1880.

21

SPEAKER'S CORNER

Karl Marx, Lenin, and George Orwell have all made speeches at Speakers' Corner, the famous bastion of free speech in Hyde Park.

22

REGENT STREET

This renowned West End street is a destination for shoppers and the facades of its listed buildings, designed by the architect John Nash, are instantly recognizable.

23

ROYAL ACADEMY OF ARTS

This private institution based in Burlington House has been promoting art and architecture since its foundation in 1768.

24

ST. JAMES'S PARK

The oldest of the royal parks lies adjacent to Buckingham Palace, and the pelicans on the banks of its lake have been a fixture here since a Russian ambassador first gifted some to Charles II in 1664.

1882
PALL MALL SW1

ABOVE

This elegant barber's shop on St. James's Street dates back to 1805 and has counted amongst its clientele such luminaries as Oscar Wilde and Winston Churchill.

OPPOSITE

St. James's Palace lies between Pall Mall and The Mall and was commissioned by Henry VIII in 1531 on the site of a former leper colony from the 12th century.

DESIGN

ALFIES ANTIQUE MARKET

A MECCA FOR BARGAIN HUNTERS

Forget the market on Portobello Road and head for Church Street, where you will find one of the largest covered antiques markets in London. Bargain hunters and discerning collectors of vintage gear have been coming to Alfies since the 1970s. Time seems to have stood still here.

Church Street, a stone's throw from the busy streets of Marylebone, has acquired a solid reputation amongst collectors; with its fifteen or so galleries, an annual festival and in particular Alfies Antique Market, this street linking Paddington Green and Lisson Grove has become an essential stop for lovers of painting, design, and fine art from the 17th century to the present day.

In 1976, journalist Bennie Gray decided to give Jordan's, a run-down old haberdasher's and department store, a new lease of life, and on the advice of his father Alfie, with whom he used to visit the antique stalls on Church Street every Saturday, he transformed the building (which he named after his father) into an antiques market. His portfolio has since expanded to include oriental arts from AlFayez on the first floor and jewelry from Gray's, another Mayfair stalwart.

Nearly ninety mini shops nestle behind its Art Deco facade decorated with Egyptian frescoes, and you can enjoy getting lost in this labyrinth of more than 32,300 square feet (3,000 m^2) over four floors, with all kinds of nooks and crannies in and around the stairwells. This inviting melting pot is home to dealers in art, rare books, mid-century modern furniture, 18th-century French discoveries, unique lamps, antique Louis Vuitton trunks, vintage African textiles, and dresses from the Roaring Twenties, not to mention the only boutique in the country dedicated to vintage Christmas decorations. There is even a shark hanging from their latest space, known as the Sharkade. Some have been here since the outset of this uniquely eclectic place, such as Linda Bee, whose Aladdin's cave is crammed with incredible 1970s jewelry, headscarves, and accessories of every kind. There are also artisan workshops amongst the merchants; picture-framers, a watchmaker from Turkey, even a Japanese ceramicist; in its thickly carpeted corridors all four corners of the world are represented in "carefully organized chaos", as our guide Alysha Woodey, who is in charge of Alfies' publicity, notes with a smile.

Try not to turn up with too many preconceived ideas or too tight a schedule to explore this treasure trove that delights Londoners, stylists, interior decorators, and prop-makers alike, not to mention tourists who have done their research. To round off your visit, head for the rooftop café for a well-earned coffee to the relaxing strains of classical music.

Vintage lovers of every kind will find what they are looking for at Alfies.

Ersan the watchmaker meticulously repairs alarm clocks, watches, and timepieces of all kinds in his shop.

Every literary taste is catered for, from history to first editions of Sherlock Holmes.

Charles' stall is crammed with rare volumes of poetry, travelogues, and cookery books.

This picture-framer's, hidden away in the corner of a corridor, is one of the market's many gems.

Every floor has its own share of unexpected discoveries.

Old rugs from the 19th century to vintage trinkets from the 1930s: you will find everything here.

Some stalls mix and match genres, as here, where watches and pictures coexist happily.

Michael sells Christmas decorations from all the countries of the former USSR.

GOETHE

ABOVE

Every member of the Royal Academy of Arts is an artist whose work has been acknowledged by their peers.

OPPOSITE

The Royal Academy of Arts summer exhibition is an unmissable fixture in London's cultural diary and an opportunity to discover new talents.

Between Hyde Park and St. James's Park, Green Park is prized for its natural simplicity in the heart of the city.

FOOD AND DRINK

THE FLAVORS OF CHINATOWN

AN ENCLAVE IN THE CENTER OF TOWN

Chinatown, the iconic epicenter of Chinese culture, extends over several streets around Gerrard Street in the West End.

STUNNING SHOP WINDOWS

The grocery stores are full of hard-to-find specialties from every corner of Asia.

STEAMED TREATS

Practice your chopstick skills for the delicious filled *xiao long bao* in broth.

FESTIVE GARLANDS

These red lanterns are synonymous with celebrations like Chinese New Year and are said to bring good luck.

FOR SHARING

The restaurants have a wide range of regional Chinese cuisines on offer, and you can order for the whole table.

BEIJING IN LONDON

Ready-to-eat Peking ducks on display in a shop window.

CHAR SIU BAO

These steamed buns from Fujian are traditionally stuffed with pork and enjoyed piping hot.

ASIAN SHOPS

You will find every fresh product for Asian cooking here, from vegetables and shellfish to fish and meat.

ABOVE

This unicorn, one of the heraldic symbols of the United Kingdom, sits proudly atop the entrance gates to Buckingham Palace.

OPPOSITE

You can watch the traditional Changing of the Guard in front of Buckingham Palace on four mornings a week.

DEEP DIVE

TEA

With 165 million cups drunk every day, the British love of tea is in no doubt and indeed has become a key part of the country's image. Tea is a mainstay of British civilization, according to the writer George Orwell, but the renowned "cuppa" comes from a land far away!

Camellia sinensis, the tea plant, originated in China and use of the leaves dates back millennia. The Middle Kingdom began to export its leaves throughout Asia in the 10th century but the first tea chests were not unloaded in European ports, of which the first was Amsterdam, until the 17th century.

Tea began to appear in City coffee houses in the 1650s and the first teahouses emerged at the turn of the 18th century, including Twinings Tea Shop, which is still to be found at 216 the Strand. The Cutty Sark in Greenwich, the fastest sailboat of its time, is a last vestige of the tea clipper era. Such boats would take to the seas under full sail and race to deliver the first harvest of the year safely into port. The Cutty Sark used to carry up to 10,000 chests of tea on every voyage.

When Catherine of Braganza married King Charles II in 1662, the Portuguese princess brought within her trousseau a chest of tea. She went on to popularize her favorite drink (already well established amongst the Portuguese upper classes) with the nobility of England. Serving such an expensive commodity to one's guests soon became an ostentatious display of wealth.

The growing popularity of tea (combined with prohibitive customs duty) quickly gave rise to smuggling and, to put a stop to this illicit trade, Parliament passed the Commutation Act of 1784. With tariffs reduced from 119 to 12.5 percent, the Tea Tax made the precious leaves more accessible and the drink (often sweetened with milk and sugar) gradually percolated into every level of society. The spread of tea culture throughout the Empire (India and Ceylon, for example) in the 18th century helped to diversify sources of supply.

In under two centuries, the entire United Kingdom was drinking tea, each in their particular way, and the very chic afternoon tea was supposedly instigated by Anna Russell, the Duchess of Bedford. To bridge the gap between lunch and dinner, the aristocrat would assemble company for "five o'clock tea", enjoyed with a spread of cakes and sandwiches. Afternoon tea has become synonymous with luxury hotels, cucumber sandwiches, and aristocratic ritual ever since. In the West Country of England, tea is accompanied by scones with jam and clotted cream, to create the famous cream tea.High tea, the name given to supper by the working classes, is taken around 6 p.m. with a cuppa, its affectionate nickname.

The domestic tea ritual has been raised to the level of national art and is still practiced in British society at all hours of the day. Even if consumption has declined in recent years in favor of herbal teas, black tea will forever remain quintessentially British. One essential debate still divides the country, however: milk or tea in first?

THE TEA PLANT

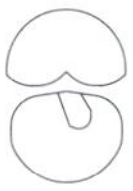

1

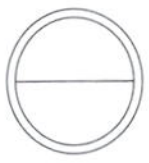

2

3

4

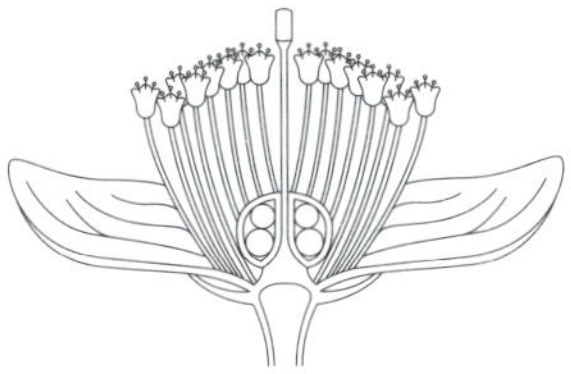

5

6

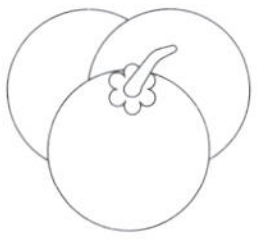

7

TEA PLANT
Camellia sinensis

ANATOMY OF A TEA PLANT

1 Embryo **2** Cross-section of seed **3** Pistil **4** Transverse cross-section of ovary
5 Longitudinal cross-section of flower **6/7** Ripe fruit seen from various angles

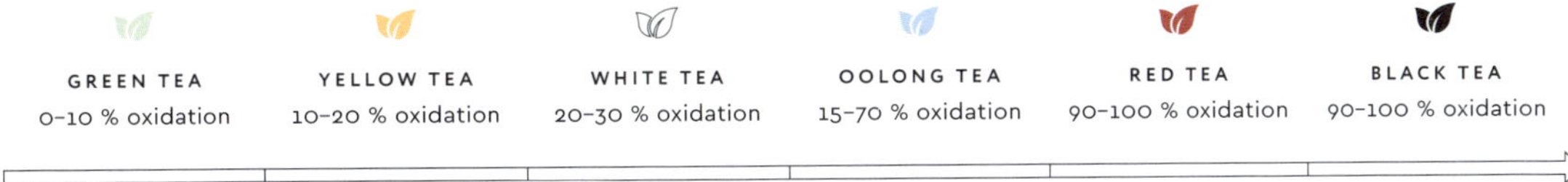

THE PROCESS OF OXIDATION AND ITS EFFECT ON TEA

ABOVE

The rooms of this five-star hotel on Grosvenor Square overlook the bell tower of a Romanesque revival church built by Alfred Waterhouse in 1891.

OPPOSITE

The luxurious Art Deco Claridge's hotel opened in the 1850s epitomizes the discreet elegance of the Mayfair district.

DAVIES STREET W1

FASHION

KNATCHBULL

LADIES ONLY ON SAVILE ROW

Daisy Knatchbull has been breaking down barriers in the legendary street of tailors in Mayfair since 2019, challenging what has been a bastion of bespoke menswear since the end of the 18th century. With the largest display window in Savile Row, her shop has rapidly established itself as the go-to for women's clothing in London.

It all started with a morning suit worn to the races at Royal Ascot, a key social event in the diaries of Britain's social elite. In 2016, Daisy Knatchbull turned up to the royal enclosure (with its immutable dress code that has stood for a century) in top hat and tails; her audacity made waves, but also opened the door to women wearing trousers.

A minor revolution, but it pushed London into rethinking bespoke tailoring, traditionally the preserve of male outfitters. Historically, these had found "female bodies too difficult, too different from each other", she explains. Ah well! The Deck (since renamed Knatchbull) was launched in 2019 and its bespoke creations, carefully designed by an all-woman team, could be ordered in more than a thousand fabrics, with custom lining, discreet embroidery, and all kinds of extras.

Style, comfort, and versatility are at the heart of Daisy Knatchbull's approach; "There is nothing worse than a beautiful piece that is uncomfortable!" she points out, so her trousers feature buckles that adjust to follow the dip and curve of body shapes, while weights in the back vent of her jackets ensure a perfect fit in all conditions.

After three months of tailoring, her bespoke creations, cut to the millimeter, became more mismatched, more relaxed, dressier, taking their owners from morning into evening. A Bianca Jagger-style wedding suit, a double-breasted corduroy jacket, a linen outfit – all these met with immediate success as her creations were adopted by Kate Moss, Gillian Anderson, and Lauren Hutton. The brand has since expanded, with silk blouses, cashmere and trench coats joining the ready-to-wear line in response to customer demand.

The label took off thanks to the pandemic, and Knatchbull left Chelsea for Savile Row, the mecca of British tailoring. Ensconced in her HQ at no. 32, the thirty-something considers her fashion house to be a bright and welcoming cocoon, the antithesis of its male counterpart, all dark wood and up-front intimidation. This was a winning bet for Britain's first B Corp-certified tailor, with more than 2,500 clients and some 1,200 bespoke suits completed each year. The founder's favorite is a pinstripe three-piece, to be worn with trainers and a white t-shirt. Smart yet casual, it is a nod to the uniform of the finance bros, bankers, and traders of the City and a sartorial breath of fresh air.

1/ DAISY KNATCHBULL

Founder Daisy Knatchbull strikes a pose in front of her display window on Savile Row.

2/ CHECKED TWEED

The pattern much beloved of Britain's high society is displayed as a total look here.

3/ EVENING DRESS

As night falls, the torch is passed on to these elegant tuxedos.

4/ INTEGRATED CLOTHING

Jackets, jumpers, and blouses complete the signature Knatchbull wardrobe.

ABOVE

The unmistakable chimes of an ice cream van are a classic feature of British park life.

OPPOSITE

Wisteria-clad Serpentine Lodge was built in the 1830s and is one of Hyde Park's many hidden treasures.

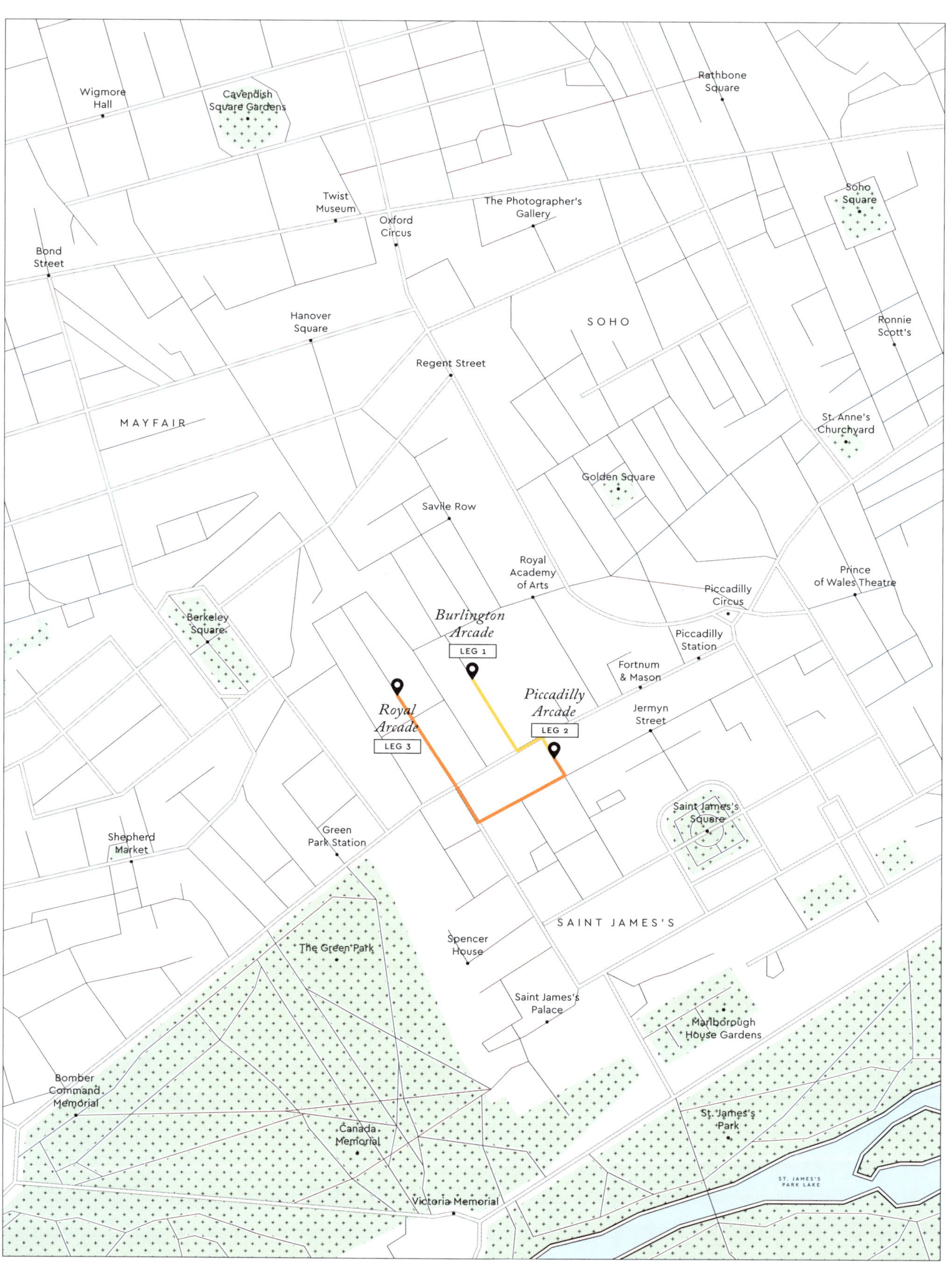
Wigmore Hall
Cavendish Square Gardens
Rathbone Square
Soho Square
Twist Museum
The Photographer's Gallery
Oxford Circus
Bond Street
Hanover Square
SOHO
Ronnie Scott's
Regent Street
MAYFAIR
St. Anne's Churchyard
Golden Square
Savile Row
Royal Academy of Arts
Prince of Wales Theatre
Piccadilly Circus
Berkeley Square
Burlington Arcade
LEG 1
Piccadilly Station
Fortnum & Mason
Piccadilly Arcade
LEG 2
Royal Arcade
LEG 3
Jermyn Street
Saint James's Square
Green Park Station
Shepherd Market
SAINT JAMES'S
Spencer House
The Green Park
Saint James's Palace
Marlborough House Gardens
Bomber Command Memorial
St. James's Park
Canada Memorial
ST. JAMES'S PARK LAKE
Victoria Memorial

WALKING TOUR

THE COVERED ARCADES

Paris's covered arcades, the forerunners of shopping malls, quickly crossed the Channel before spreading pretty much throughout Europe. Some of the most flamboyant specimens of these temples of London elegance, all of which are listed buildings, are located in the fashionable area of Mayfair.

LEG 1 : BURLINGTON ARCADE

London's first covered arcade sprang up between Green Park and Piccadilly stations in 1819, under the guidance of Lord George Cavendish, 1st Earl of Burlington, linking Piccadilly with Burlington Gardens. His commission charged architect Samuel Ware to create a gallery "for the sale of jewelry and fancy articles of fashionable demand" and since then, the longest covered arcade in the country has been home to all the must-haves of British luxury goods under its 587-ft (179-m) glass roof. Jewelers, fashion houses, and sophisticated pastry sellers rub shoulders with expert shoeshiners and even the reseller of the largest collection of secondhand Rolexes in the world. One anachronistic oddity that is not to be missed are the three beadles, officials in frock coats and top hats, who uphold Victorian tradition by making sure than no passer-by "sings, whistles, runs, holds an open umbrella or carries bulky parcels" in the arcade.

LEG 2 : PICCADILLY ARCADE

Leave the Burlington Arcade at the Piccadilly end and cross the road to enter Piccadilly Arcade, which will take you onto Jermyn Street. This jewel of London architecture on the border of Mayfair and St. James's opened in 1909 to a design by architect George Thrale Jell and is a perfect example of the opulent style of the Edwardian era. The office spaces created above the shops are still there. Admire the glazed jade and cream mosaic floor and explore the 16 boutiques decorated with stylized balustrades and curving ironwork. Behind their black and gold shop windows, you will find traditional tailors, shoemakers, antiques dealers, perfumiers, delicatessens, and bakeries beneath the ornate domes, a mix of tradition and innovation that is wholly in the spirit of the first boutiques to be established here.

LEG 3 : ROYAL ARCADE

Returning to Piccadilly, take a right into Old Bond Street to explore the Royal Arcade, which will take you onto Albemarle Street. The arcade was built by architect G. Smith in 1879, and its regal name is due to one of the very first businesses here, the shirtmaker H. W. Brettell, an official supplier to Queen Victoria in the 1880s who attracted a refined clientele to the arcade. It is a typical example of Victorian architecture and has changed little over almost 150 years, housing jewelers, perfumiers, chocolate-makers, antiques dealers, and art galleries. Amongst its original features, keep an eye out for the curving windows, Ionic columns, and imposing decorative stucco arches. Lavish Christmas decorations make it a popular stroll at the end of the year, and for a 100 percent Art Deco experience, enjoy a bite to eat amongst the marble columns of The Wolseley, a little further down at 160 Piccadilly, a grandiose European café.

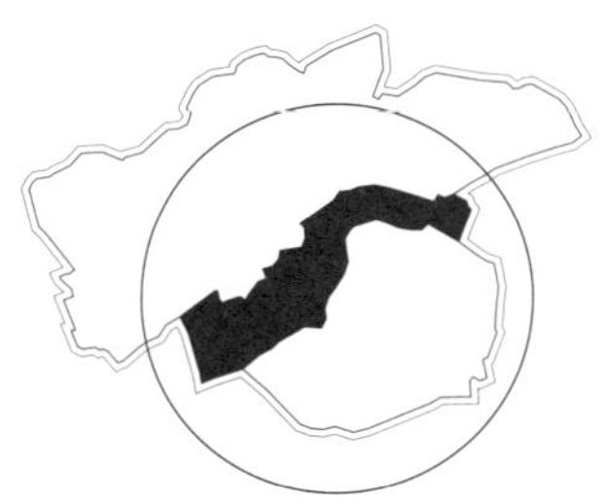

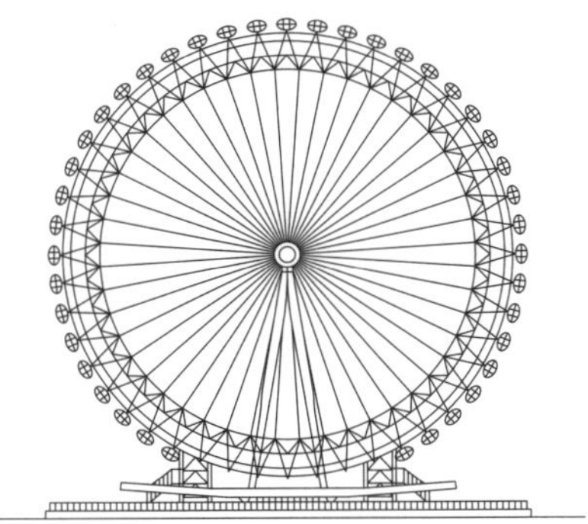

FROM THE BANKS OF THE THAMES TO THE HEART OF LONDON

RIVERBANKS

Passing through the heart of London, the banks of the Thames are silent witnesses to a city in perpetual flux. Along a distance of about 4½ miles (7 km) from Battersea to London Bridge (traveling from east to west), they offer an insight into the many aspects of the capital and reveal a striking contrast between industrial heritage, historic monuments, and areas of urban renewal.

P.68

The view of Westminster Palace from the south bank of the Thames is breathtaking. The Victoria Tower is 323 feet (98.5 m) high and is used to store Parliamentary records.

OPPOSITE

The Georgian house on Cardinal's Wharf at 40 Bankside was built in 1710, and the renowned architect Christopher Wren lived just a few doors down.

Once the industrial and maritime heartlands of the UK capital, the area around the Thames was long a myriad of docks and shipyards before gradually falling into disuse. Renovation projects began to transform these wastelands in the 1980s and the first major works were started in Canary Wharf (on the north bank), followed by the Southbank, as urban landscapes were reimagined as a business district and a cultural center respectively. Since the 2010s, it has been Nine Elms' turn to get a makeover, with new cosmopolitan districts popping up around the new American embassy and the iconic Battersea Power Station, a symbol of the old industrial era. Taking their cue from international predecessors, there is now a mixture of luxury condos, modern businesses, and public spaces along the waterfront.

The riverbanks are also essential features from a cultural perspective, with a concentration of major institutions on both sides of the river: Tate Britain, Tate Modern, the National Theatre, Shakespeare's Globe, and Somerset House all welcome millions of visitors every year.

The esplanade of Chelsea Embankment on the north bank is a perfect place for a stroll, and its opulent Victorian and Georgian townhouses give a real sense of British elegance. The sleepy residential district of Pimlico just next door is known for its leafy streets lined with white, Regency-style stucco facades. The atmosphere suddenly comes alive a little further north around Victoria, one of the largest stations in the city.

On a traditional note, the area around Westminster includes all the emblematic places of British power: Westminster Palace, the seat of Parliament, its famous clock, Big Ben, and Buckingham Palace are all located here. Westminster Abbey is nearby, and the London Eye looms over the opposite bank. The Tower of London to the east recalls the city's medieval past, while the bascules of Tower Bridge bear witness to the technological prowess of the Victorian era.

Last but by no means least, London Bridge is the oldest crossing point on the Thames; there was a wooden bridge in Roman times. There is a mixture of eras on the south bank, with the Gothic architecture of Southwark Cathedral rubbing shoulders with the famous Borough Market and its metal Victorian structure. All this stands in the benign shadow of the Shard, the futuristic skyscraper designed by Renzo Piano, highly visible proof of the architectural diversity that is so typical of the constantly evolving British capital.

CARDINAL'S WHARF
49

THE ESSENTIALS

25

ALBERT BRIDGE

The bridge was built in 1873 to connect Chelsea (on the north side of the Thames) with Battersea to the south.

26

BIG BEN

The clock tower, a classic symbol of London, was renamed the Elizabeth Tower in 2012 to mark the diamond jubilee of Queen Elizabeth II.

27

HMS BELFAST

This Royal Navy Town-class light cruiser moored closed to London Bridge station is a veteran of World War II.

28

BLAVATNIK BUILDING

There is a breathtaking view of the City from the terrace of the Blavatnik Building, the Tate Modern annexe.

29

ST. PAUL'S CATHEDRAL

This spectacular Anglican cathedral designed by the architect Christopher Wren is home to works by a number of contemporary artists.

30

TATE BRITAIN

This gallery on Millbank houses a large collection dedicated to British art from the 16th century to the present day.

31

BLACKFRIARS BRIDGE

The name harks back to the black vestments of the Dominicans, but the current iron bridge was designed by engineer Joseph Cubitt in 1869.

32

TOWER BRIDGE

Perhaps the most famous bridge in London. Its Gothic Revival architecture was unveiled in 1894 and the view over London's major monuments from the upper walkway is breathtaking.

33

WESTMINSTER PALACE

This palace on the north bank of the Thames is the seat of the UK Parliament, comprising the House of Commons and the House of Lords. It was rebuilt from 1840.

34

SHAKESPEARE'S GLOBE

This faithful replica of the Elizabethan theater of 1599 was the idea of American actor Sam Wanamaker and celebrates the works of William Shakespeare on a daily basis.

35

MILLENNIUM BRIDGE

This steel footbridge linking St. Paul's and Tate Modern was unveiled in 2000. It appears to float above the water.

36

TATE MODERN

The decommissioned Bankside Power Station started a new life as a museum of contemporary art of international stature in 2000.

ABOVE

Tate Britain on Millbank is the definitive museum of national art.

OPPOSITE

Designed by architect William Tite, the famous cupola of Tate Britain dominates the main entrance.

ABOVE

The superb Art Deco building of St. Olaf House on the banks of the river is now part of London Bridge Hospital.

OPPOSITE

Triptych Bankside is a new area on the south bank of the Thames behind Tate Modern and Shakespeare's Globe.

ARCHITECTURE

BATTERSEA POWER STATION

A RENEWED ENERGY

A relic of London's industrial past once more stands proud on the south bank of the Thames between Battersea Park and Vauxhall. Long abandoned, Battersea Power Station and the surrounding 40 acres (16 ha) of wasteland in Nine Elms have now been completely renovated, springing up as a new district in 2022 as the culmination of Herculean labors.

The architecture may remind you of Tate Modern and there is no wonder as it was designed by the same architect, Sir Giles Gilbert Scott, who was also responsible for Waterloo Bridge and the red telephone box. The power station was constructed in several phases, starting in 1929. At the height of its power production in the 1950s, the largest brick building in Europe (525 ft/160 m in length and 358 ft/109 m high) was providing nearly 20 percent of the city's energy and consuming 10,000 tonnes of coal every week.

The power station is an urban and cultural icon, making its most famous appearance on the sleeve of the Pink Floyd album *Animals* (1977). To get the shot, the band suspended Algie, a giant inflatable pig, between the two north chimneys. The pig unfortunately broke free, wreaking havoc with that day's air traffic.

The station slowly fell into disuse, gradually shutting down its turbines before coming to a complete halt in 1983. Several renewal projects came to nothing before a takeover by a Malaysian consortium in 2014. The group wants to revitalize this abandoned area in the heart of the capital and, eight years and nine billion pounds later, an entire neighborhood has emerged from the wasteland.

A gargantuan, eight-phase project was entrusted to renowned architectural partnerships that included WilkinsonEyre, dRMM, Gehry Partners, and Foster + Partners. Just restoring the station from top to bottom (it has since been listed) required the manufacture of 1.75 million bricks for the structure and more than 25,000 barrowloads of concrete to repair each of its four fluted chimneys. Starting in 2017, apartments, offices (including Apple's London headquarters), shops, hanging gardens, a cinema, 22,000 square feet (2,000 m^2) of food courts, and even a new Tube station have been gradually added.

People now come to the power station to relax with a book in a deckchair, enjoy a stroll in the gardens, dine on the waterside terrace or mooch from one boutique to the next. Look out for Turbine A in this colossal edifice (its impressive original structure and meticulously restored Art Deco detailing are worth the detour) before heading to Lift 109. A glass elevator nestling in the bowels of the northwest chimney will take you to the summit, and during the ascent you can witness a spectacular panoramic view of the capital, including the skyline from the MI6 building to Hampton Court Palace, taking in the Royal Observatory at Greenwich and the Millennium Bridge.

The sheer size of the power station is best appreciated from the opposite bank.

Contemporary luxury apartment buildings have sprung up around the power station.

The highly exclusive penthouses on the roof terrace come with a private garden.

Colored flags were hung in the turbine room for a temporary installation.

The glass elevator rises 358 feet (109 m) on its journey up the center of the northwest chimney.

A series of hand-painted picnic tables were designed by Adalberto Lonardi.

The original Art Deco detailing has been preserved, such as these fluted columns.

The famous chimneys look out over the entire neighborhood.

Bricks and steel are ubiquitous in the power station's architecture.

P.80–81

On a clear day, enjoy a picture-postcard view from the south bank of the Thames of the City skyscrapers.

ABOVE

This famous Ferris wheel, which opened in 2000, is known as the London Eye.

OPPOSITE

Don't bother looking for glass pod number 13; it has been superstitiously omitted.

ART

SOMERSET HOUSE

ART AND INNOVATION

There are many excellent reasons to come to Somerset House, on the north bank of the Thames, largely thanks to its visionary director. Let's meet Jonathan Reekie CBE, who has succeeded in making this historic building an innovative and creative artistic hub and a mecca for contemporary London culture.

"Supporting all the creative talents of our time by offering them a space where they can meet and experiment right in the heart of the city" is the guiding principle espoused by Reekie, who has headed the Somerset House Trust since 2014. After working at the Aldeburgh Festival of classical music on the Suffolk coast, he brought his influence to bear on this institution, which was seeking a clear and defined direction. Once the residence of the dukes of Somerset and then a public records office, the 18th-century Neoclassical building was not designed to accommodate the public (its now legendary central courtyard was even used as a parking lot for civil servants!) so everything had to be reinvented.

Somerset House is not a museum or a traditional arts center. Reekie has transformed it into an epicenter of innovation and contemporary creativity dedicated to multidisciplinary arts, blurring the boundaries of "what art should be".

With an ear always open to the younger generation, the director undertook major renovations to woo them, and an unparalleled laboratory has emerged over the years, serving artists, artisans, start-ups, researchers, entrepreneurs, companies with social aims, and much more. From fashion to artificial intelligence, from music to design, a whole industry of creatives has now gathered on the Strand, and with more than 2,000 people in residence, it is the largest community of its kind in the United Kingdom. "I love to see ideas cross paths before they develop; they never thrive on their own, but they are nourished through the interaction of creative minds. It is this emulation that we support on a daily basis as we link up creation and production", he explains.

This creative hurly-burly strikes a natural chord with the cutting-edge but inclusive curation at Somerset House, which is aimed at a discerning and diverse audience. With workshops, performances, and themed exhibitions, their programming plays with categories and is not afraid to keep asking the big questions of our times, such as with the recent *Cute*, *24/7*, and *Big Data*. The central courtyard becomes an open-air venue for a host of events and the list is endless: immersive installations, an ice rink, movie screenings, concerts, family activities. The building also houses the Impressionist collection of the highly reputed Courtauld Institute of Art, along with several carefully selected cafés and restaurants.

So what's the next challenge as its twenty-fifth year of operation comes around? "To make the world understand our very essence", he concludes with a grin, having recently been decorated as a Commander of the Order of the British Empire (CBE) for services to culture.

Temporary exhibitions are dedicated to major fashion retrospectives.

Somerset House's monumental central courtyard is filled with life during events.

The residential studios are tucked away in the bowels of this giant Victorian building.

A bronze statue of King George III stands at the entrance to the central courtyard.

Visitors stop off for a break in the elegant WatchHouse coffee shop in the east wing.

The gift shop space is sometimes given a makeover by a prominent artist.

Some 2.7 million visitors pass through Somerset House every year.

Director Jonathan Reekie CBE strikes a pose in the central courtyard.

As you leave Somerset House, you will see the church of St. Mary le Strand to your right.

DEEP DIVE

THE THAMES

For the best view of London's spectacular skyline, simply cross the Thames on the top deck of a double-decker bus or take to the water on a river bus. Rising in the south of England and flowing into the North Sea, the 58-million-year-old river is intimately bound up with the history of the capital.

The second-longest river in the country is 215 miles (346 km) long, of which a 42-mile (68-km) stretch flows through Greater London, from Hampton Court in the west to the Isle of Dogs in the east, before it meets the Thames Barrier that protects it from flooding. Locals have enjoyed the benefits of this strategic natural resource since the Neolithic period, with water use, energy, international trade, and even culinary traditions dependent on its flow. In the 18th century, jellied eels became part of the diet of the poorest Londoners and the famed pie, mash, and eel shops began to make an appearance in the East End, such as the iconic M. Manze shop from 1902.

Thanks to its water of varying salinity and a scattering of eighty islands and eyots, the Thames is home to a rich ecosystem of more than a hundred or so species, with cormorants, seabirds, gulls, and swans nesting on its banks, and saltwater and freshwater fish mingling in its waters. A colony of seals has even taken up residence near the estuary. In the 1250s, it was apparently common to see Henry III's polar bear (a present from King Haakon of Norway) fishing nearby!

The Thames has not always been a long, quiet river, however, and the stretch from its source to Teddington Lock, west of London is punctuated by forty-five locks; only the last section to the estuary is tidal. At London Bridge, the water level may vary by anything from 18 to 23 feet (5.5 to 7 m) between spring and neap tides. After several instances of sea floods, of which the storm surge of 1953 was the most grievous, the United Kingdom erected the second-largest barrage in the world (after the Oosterscheldekering in the Netherlands) in 1984 to counter floodwater from the North Sea. The retro-futuristic design of the Thames Barrier (the work of engineer Charles Draper from Rendel, Palmer and Tritton) sparkles just downstream from central London, and in the event of a flood risk, its ten rotating gates will hold back the rising seawater. They can then be lowered as the tide recedes to release the water.

The Thames has been immortalized in the paintings of William Turner, who was able to capture its shifting light like no other, but has also inspired other artists, including Jason deCaires Taylor, an eco-sculptor whose temporary installation of 2015 entitled *The Rising Tide* was made up of four horses that were visible only at low tide. The embankments of the Thames are popular places to stroll in London and the river is a big draw for water sports, with rowing, that most British of disciplines, the most popular by far!

ECLECTIC BRIDGES

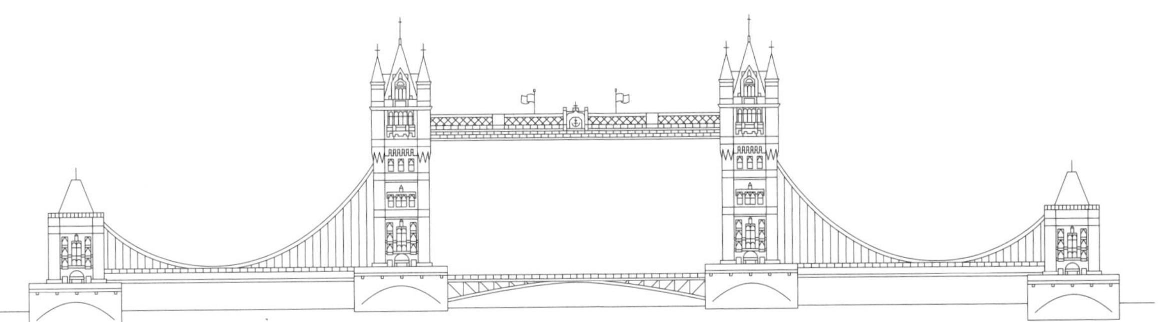

TOWER BRIDGE

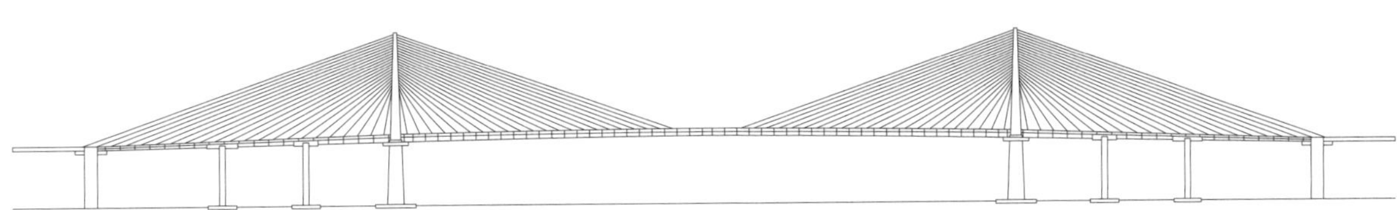

QUEEN ELIZABETH II BRIDGE

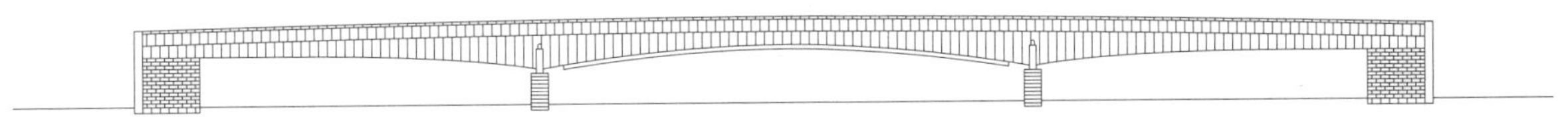

LONDON BRIDGE

WESTMINSTER BRIDGE

ABOVE

The statue of Queen Anne erected on the forecourt of St. Paul's to mark the completion of the cathedral's construction has been welcoming visitors since 1712.

OPPOSITE

The impressive dome of St. Paul's weighs nearly 65,000 tonnes and dominates the city.

WELCOME TO LONDON

ABOVE

These concrete pillars at the base of Tate Modern are exposed with each low tide.

OPPOSITE

Beaches are revealed at low tide, such as this one alongside Paul's Walk, and mudlarkers set about sifting the mud and sand for treasures.

ABOVE

The bell tower of St. Dunstan in the East was an addition by Christopher Wren and survived the Blitz.

OPPOSITE

...and there was light; through the poetic ruins of St. Dunstan in the East.

NATURE

SWIMMING THE ENGLISH WAY

365 DAYS A YEAR

Taking their example from Lord Byron, Londoners go wild swimming throughout the year, come rain or shine!

WEST RESERVOIR CENTRE

This former reservoir built in 1833 has now been adapted for swimming and water sports.

HIGHGATE MEN'S POND

There are three swimming ponds on Hampstead Heath: ladies', men's, and mixed.

LONDON FIELDS LIDO

This heated pool has been delighting East London swimmers since 1931.

SERPENTINE LIDO

The Serpentine Swimming Club of Hyde Park is the oldest swimming club in the country, and is open from May to October.

OPEN WATER CANARY WHARF

Amid the offices, the Middle Lock on Canary Wharf welcomes swimmers in a basin between two locks.

WILD SWIMMING

Fans of swimming in natural surroundings can take to the ponds of Hampstead Heath.

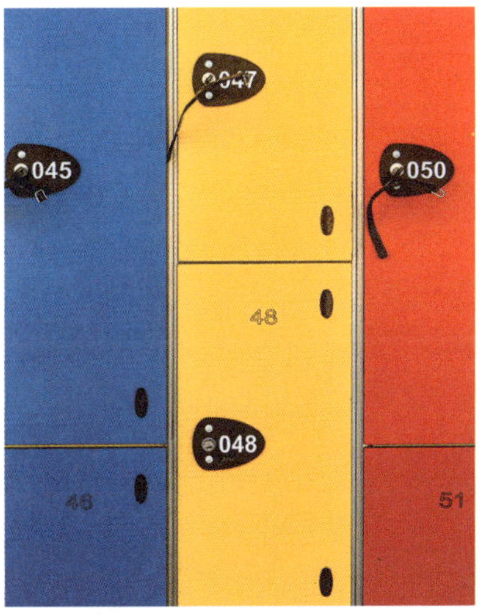

TECHNICOLOR

The lockers beside the pool at London Fields Lido are part of the decor.

PARLIAMENT HILL LIDO

If you don't mind the cold, enjoy a dip in this open-air pool in the north of the capital, which is open all year round.

ABOVE

Westminster Palace was rebuilt in a Gothic style by architect Charles Barry after a devastating fire in 1834. It is listed as a UNESCO World Heritage site.

OPPOSITE

This walkway beneath Westminster Bridge has a breathtaking view of Big Ben.

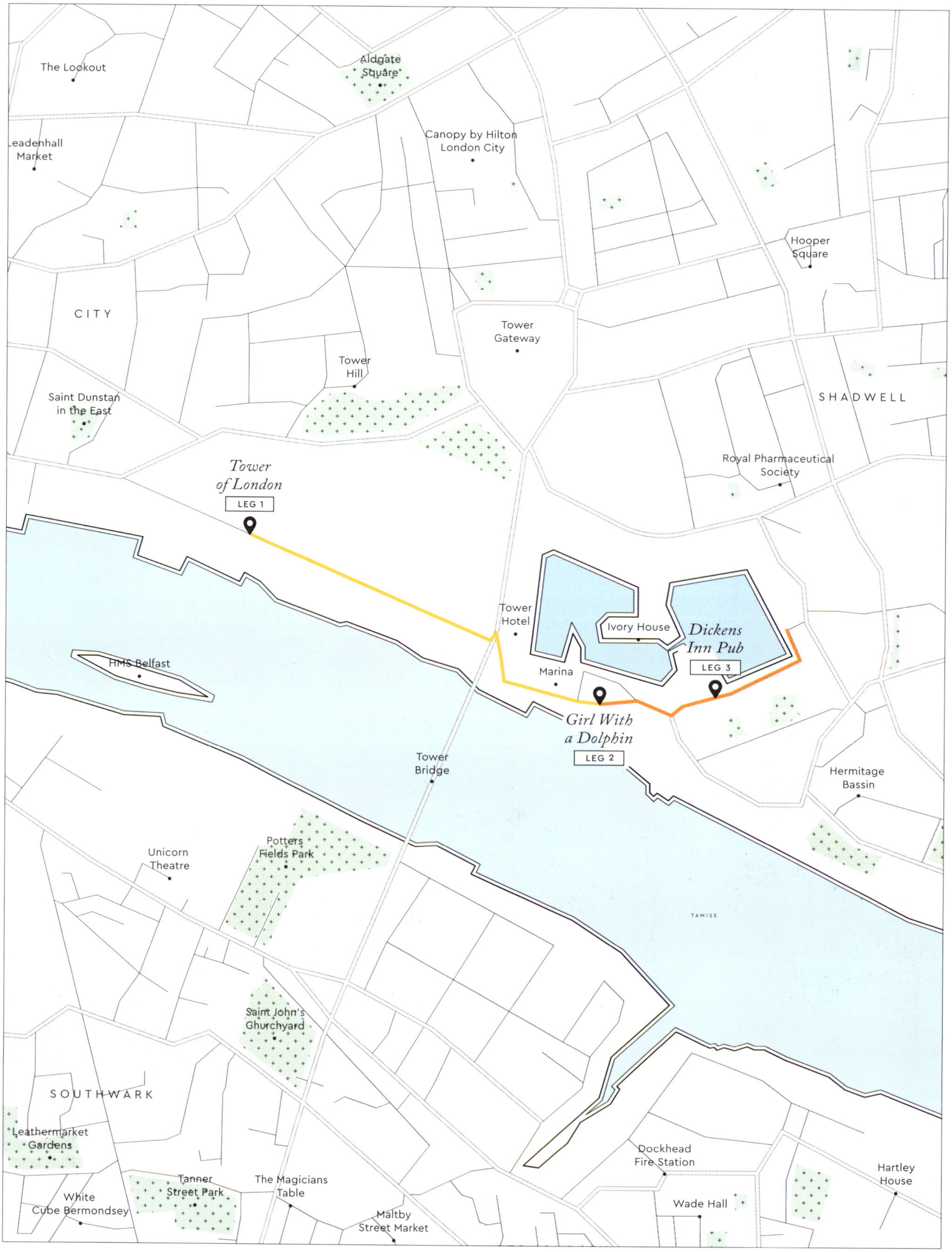

The Lookout
Aldgate Square
Leadenhall Market
Canopy by Hilton London City
Hooper Square
CITY
Tower Gateway
Tower Hill
Saint Dunstan in the East
SHADWELL
Royal Pharmaceutical Society
Tower of London
LEG 1
Tower Hotel
Ivory House
Dickens Inn Pub
LEG 3
HMS Belfast
Marina
Girl With a Dolphin
LEG 2
Tower Bridge
Hermitage Bassin
Unicorn Theatre
Potters Fields Park
TAMISE
Saint John's Churchyard
SOUTHWARK
Leathermarket Gardens
Dockhead Fire Station
Hartley House
Tanner Street Park
The Magicians Table
White Cube Bermondsey
Wade Hall
Maltby Street Market

WALKING TOUR

ST. KATHARINE DOCKS

Head east along the north bank of the Thames from the tourists thronging the Tower of London and you will reach the only marina in the center of the capital. Once a medieval hospital, St. Katharine Docks now boasts a quayside and a marina with bars and restaurants and has the feel of a small village far away from the hustle and bustle of the city.

LEG 1 : THE THAMES PATH TOWARD THE MARINA

Nothing beats arriving at St. Katharine Docks by water, so first take the River Bus to Tower Millennium Pier. Now head east along the Thames Path past the Tower of London and pick up the next section of this riverside walk. The brutalist Tower Hotel awaits you to the left. Voted the second most-hated building in London in a BBC survey of 2006, this concrete cruise liner was designed by the British architects Renton Howard Wood Partnership as part of a redevelopment of the area in the 1970s. Many of London's iconic buildings are reflected in its bay windows. This is also the spot from which to take a look behind you as the view of Tower Bridge is spectacular.

LEG 2 : THE OLD DOCKS

Passing by David Wynne's sculpture *Girl with a Dolphin*, you will cross a footbridge over the lock to reach the marina. This former dock was designed by the engineer Thomas Telford and opened in 1828. Its layout featuring a lock with interconnected basins enabled efficient unloading of tea, tobacco, ivory, spices, and other goods into the warehouses. The dock was partially destroyed by German bombing during World War II and the port was gradually abandoned before all commercial activity was halted in 1968. The real estate developers Taylor Woodrow then set about revamping the docks for the general public.

LEG 3 : THE CURRENT ROLE OF THE MARINA

Take a left past the old Dockmaster's office. The reinvention of the docks as a marina was completed in the 1990s, and there is a surprisingly calm atmosphere here in the heart of the city, broken only by the clock of Ivory House, a red-brick warehouse that survived the Blitz, and the dip and sway of yachts and motorboats lying peacefully on their moorings. To the right, admire the wooden facade of the Dickens Inn on its brick base. It was rebuilt in the style of a Victorian inn during the redevelopment, when the original building was moved 77 yards/70 m to the east! This is an ideal stop for a pint with a fantastic view of the basins. If you are more interested in coffee shops, fresh pasta, seafood, or tacos, there is no shortage of options in and around the marina. Finish your stroll around the east basin, passing the apartments of City Quay and the South Quay Estate. If you visit in September, you will come across the Classic Boat Festival with its workshops, concerts, and a range of nautical activities, along with about forty vintage boats in the basins.

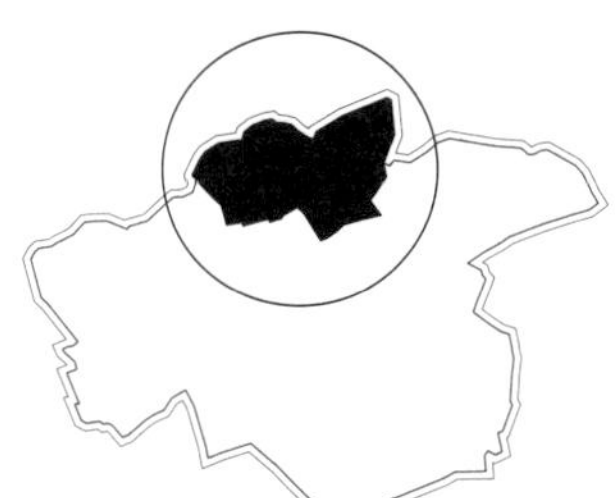

CAMDEN, HAMPSTEAD, ISLINGTON, LITTLE VENICE, KING'S CROSS, PRIMROSE HILL, REGENT'S PARK, STOKE NEWINGTON

NORTH

Green spaces, a creative atmosphere, a blend of classical and contemporary architecture: these are just some of the charms of these neighborhoods. From indie gigs in Camden to the elegant homes of Hampstead, taking in the reinvigorated industrial spirit of King's Cross and the village-like atmosphere of Primrose Hill, north London is a patchwork that reflects the vibrant soul of the city.

P.100

Little Venice is the ideal spot to admire the colorful narrowboats that line the canals.

OPPOSITE

With its pretty facades, neat squares, and charming local pubs, residential Barnsbury is a tranquil little corner that is the perfect place for a stroll.

The area of King's Cross Central to the north of the former freight hub of King's Cross is unrecognizable today. After the frenetic nightlife of the 1980s, its disused warehouses have now been transformed into a fashionable district of designer boutiques and restaurants, delicatessens, cutting-edge office spaces, and residential apartments in the old "gasometers" (gas holders) along the Regent's Canal. The old coal store yard of Coal Drops Yard was unveiled in 2018 as a lifestyle complex of a kind the UK capital has a knack for, while the artists from Central Saint Martins College of Art and Design live alongside tech bros from the neighboring offices in the environs of Granary Square.

As you follow the canal, Camden slowly unfolds its indie atmosphere. The area is renowned for its music scene, from the Electric Ballroom to the Roundhouse, and its links with artists like Amy Winehouse and The Clash, but it is also a haven for street art and vintage clothing, and the murals and eclectic stalls of Camden Market attract tourists from around the world.

The atmosphere changes radically at Regent's Park, a green haven. The park was designed by architect John Nash in the 19th century, and its meticulously kept gardens, lake, zoo, open-air theater, and festivals make it an unmissable stop. The white stucco homes of Cumberland Terrace to the southeast (also by Nash) are amongst the most prestigious addresses in the city.

Primrose Hill a little to the north has a peaceful and village-like atmosphere. Perched atop a rise with breathtaking views, the area boasts cobbled mews, cozy cafés, and charming houses with pastel facades, and it is very popular with Londoners looking for calm and privacy. The same is true of Hampstead, a short distance away, whose vast villas and bucolic charm make it a popular bolt hole for celebrities. Hampstead Heath's 790 acres (320 ha) of parkland are a unique haven close to the city center.

Last but not least, Islington, farther to the east, incorporates the transition between the city center and the creative neighborhoods of Hackney. Once a rural village, it is now home to a population of well-heeled intellectuals looking for carefree elegance. The secluded enclaves of Barnsbury and Canonbury are a typical mix of Georgian terraces and Victorian townhouses lining charming leafy streets. Theaters such as the King's Head and the Almeida join the area's restaurants and small boutiques in making Islington a must-visit destination.

BARNSBURY
ROAD, N.1.
118A

THE ESSENTIALS

37

THE BRITISH LIBRARY

One of the greatest libraries in the world is notably home to two of the four existing copies of the Magna Carta and handwritten Beatles song lyrics.

38

PRIMROSE HILL

The view over London from the brow of the hill in this 62-acre (25-ha) park located north of Regent's Park is breathtaking.

39

CITY ROAD LOCK

The City Lock Basin on the Regent's Canal is a popular stopping point for a moment by the river.

40

CAMDEN

Famed for its market and alternative culture, Camden is also one of the capital's music hotspots.

41

HAMPSTEAD HEATH

This 790-acre (320-ha) oasis of greenery is the most iconic in all of north London, with unique views from Parliament Hill.

42

HAMPSTEAD VILLAGE

One of the most charming areas of London, with impressively preserved Georgian lanes.

43

CAMDEN PASSAGE

This typical small cobbled lane in Islington is home to many antique dealers.

44

LITTLE VENICE

Waterside living is popular in this timeless area at the confluence of the Grand Union Canal and the Regent's Canal.

45

ALMEIDA THEATRE

This tiny theater housed in a listed 19th-century building just off Upper Street is known for its innovative productions.

46

COAL DROPS YARD

This new shopping mall boasts about a hundred boutiques and restaurants and is part of the renewal project for the King's Cross area.

47

ST. PANCRAS STATION

The Eurostar trains that link the British capital to Paris, Lille, Brussels, and Amsterdam roll in beneath the glass roof of the Barlow train shed.

48

REGENT'S PARK

One of London's most iconic royal parks, with an area of 410 acres (166 ha). With no fewer than 400 varieties, the magnificent rose garden is worth a detour on its own.

ABOVE

Little Venice's famous small blue bridge stands at the confluence of the Grand Union and Regent's Canals.

OPPOSITE

Picturesque Little Venice is the ideal spot to admire the colorful narrowboats that line the canals; there's even a barge with a puppet theater!

DANCE

SADLER'S WELLS

OVERSEAS BALLET

Alistair Spalding's declared intent was to turn Sadler's Wells into the official home of contemporary dance in the United Kingdom and the bet has paid off for its artistic director and chief executive, who has celebrated twenty years at the head of an institution that has become a fixture.

The miraculous spring discovered by Richard Sadler in 1683 has since dried up, but it was on the site of that water source that the best of contemporary dance emerged. The birthplace of the Royal Ballet, the Birmingham Royal Ballet, and the English National Opera was rejigged exclusively for dance in the 1990s. Once past its famous red portal on Rosebery Avenue, north of Clerkenwell, the listed building (half Georgian, half glazed cube) is divided up into several spaces; the main auditorium seats 1,500 while the Baylis Studio and the rehearsal spaces are more intimate.

Alistair Spalding joined the ranks of Sadler's Wells in 2004, but it is no more than about thirty years since the artistic director and chief executive got involved in the world of culture, taking his first steps at the Hawth theater in Crawley before making a strong impression at the famous Southbank Centre. "I discovered contemporary dance when I first began and I was instantly hooked; this is an art form with the power to take you on a journey", he recalls. His clear priority from then on was to imbue the theater with a clear and powerful identity as the home of dance of all kinds.

The first step was to establish a long-term collaboration with leading British dancer and choreographer Matthew Bourne, who had won particular fame for his take on Russian ballet and his adaptation of Tim Burton's *Edward Scissorhands*. Playing this repertoire to houses that were sold out every year for twenty years made it possible to "reach a less expert audience and to popularize dance", he explains.

This was compounded by the launch of the Associate Artists program that placed dancers at the heart of the creative process, attracting major talents of the likes of Sylvie Guillem, Crystal Pite, Sidi Larbi Cherkaoui, and William Forsythe. The theater worked closely with them to co-produce and distribute new and original works, thus cementing its reputation on the international scene. Their productions traveled all over the world, including Sidi Larbi Cherkaoui's Sutra and Zero Degrees, a performance that came from the experiences of both Cherkaoui and the choreographer and dancer Akram Khan, of Bangladesh heritage. The languages of dance have been reinvented under his aegis.

His most recent project has been the opening of Sadler's Wells East, a new building in the Queen Elizabeth Olympic Park in Stratford, East London, a fantastic platform intended to continue the diversification of their audience and bring contemporary dance to the daily lives of British people from all walks of life. "Dance is a universal language! It can reach everyone, as happened to me when I was still uninitiated; this is what I hope to continue to push", he concludes.

ARTISTIC COMMUNITY

Alistair Spalding stands in front of the gallery of Associate Artists portraits in the stairwell.

A RENOWNED INSTITUTION

This cultural institution has been bringing dance right up to date in London for twenty-five years.

ABOVE

A bronze statue of British poet John Betjeman welcomes visitors to the hall of St. Pancras International.

OPPOSITE

The Gothic Revival building housing St. Pancras station was designed by George Gilbert Scott in 1868 and is also home to a luxury hotel for travelers.

ABOVE

The Regent's Canal links the renovated area of Pancras Square with Granary Square.

OPPOSITE

There is a landscaped pathway along the banks of the canal at Coal Drops Yard.

ABOVE

Residents often paint the doors of their Islington houses in bright colors.

OPPOSITE

Highbury Fields, the largest green space in Islington, is lined with fashionable houses.

Islington's highly photogenic fire station on Upper Street was designed by the architect Peter Smith in 1992.

FIRE STATION
1992
CLEAR

ARCHITECTURE

THE CEMETERIES

THE MAGNIFICENT SEVEN

The seven Victorian cemeteries were laid out like gardens and are all located within a radius of 5½ miles (9 km) as the crow flies from St. Paul's.

HIGHGATE CEMETERY

You can pay your respects at the tombs of luminaries such as Karl Marx in the most famous cemeteries.

NATURE AND ARCHITECTURE

There is an element of timeless beauty in the neglect of this vault.

ABNEY PARK CEMETERY

Europe's most wooded cemetery was opened in Stoke Newington in 1840.

MONUMENTAL

This statue is an allegorical representation of faith, hope, and charity.

RENEWED INTEREST

After a long period of neglect, the cemeteries' historic and ecological importance has brought them back into the spotlight over the last twenty years.

NATURE AND ARCHITECTURE

The ivy covering the gravestones lends them a timeless atmosphere.

INSCRIPTIONS

Fans of epitaphs will enjoy deciphering the Gothic lettering of the inscriptions on some of the gravestones.

BROMPTON CEMETERY

Stroll around the tombs mixing Gothic Revival, Egyptian, and Baroque styles.

ABOVE

Stoke Newington Church Street connects Green Lanes to Stoke Newington High Street and is lined with small shops, cafés, and restaurants.

OPPOSITE

The green spaces around St. Mary's Church, in the heart of Clissold Park in Stoke Newington, are an ideal spot for a picnic.

ARTS AND CRAFTS

BELLERBY & CO.

AROUND THE WORLD IN 50 INCHES

You can now immortalize your world in a sphere 5 to 50 inches (12 to 127 cm) in diameter. In an age when digital reigns supreme, Peter Bellerby has an unapologetically artisanal approach to breathing new life into the poetry of globes, a hitherto dying art. Every model made methodically by hand in the Bellerby & Co. workshop in Stoke Newington is unique.

This former warehouse tucked away in a dead end just a stone's throw from Stoke Newington Church Street was converted into a workshop in 2012. Four years earlier, Peter Bellerby had created a bespoke globe himself for his father's eightieth birthday after finding no one who could make it for him. It took him hundreds of failed attempts to master a trade that, according to the Heritage Crafts association, had fallen into oblivion and was in danger of extinction in the United Kingdom as it was no longer being taught anywhere.

"You have to be prepared to fail often. I took two years to create my first model", laughs the new artisan, who has always preferred learning by experience. A decade later, his autodidactic spirit has spread throughout the entire workshop of around thirty co-workers. The first floor is a riot of wood, metal, resin, and even fiberglass, the materials needed for making the globes, mounts, and prototypes, but this leads on out into the light of another world; the glazed open space in the attic is full of cartographers, painters and illustrators, surrounded by vintage furniture, old rugs, and green plants, all working in a shared silence.

"The key thing in our job is patience, closely followed by an extreme delicate touch in handling materials, precise dexterity, and a keen eye. Initially, it was yoga that taught me how to move my body deliberately. Learning to slow down is essential; you have to understand the limitations of rolls of paper and try not to exceed them", Peter explains.

Bellerby & Co.'s terrestrial and celestial globes, with their infinite poetry, are all handmade and each one is totally unique. Around 500 units are made every year, of which three-quarters are bespoke orders; a simple illustration, markings of specific routes, hundreds of personalized drawings. Depending on the complexity of the project, the watercolor phase can last from ten days to more than a month for a globe 26 inches (65 cm) in diameter.

"Using roads to tell stories is the most moving part of my job", confides the firm's founder. Somewhere between an aide-memoire and a legacy, his globes are an excuse to record a lifetime's knowledge and hand it down for future generations. A family may retrace the exodus of previous generations, a rock group can revisit its tours, geologists explain their work on Icelandic glaciers. This is just a glimpse of the reason customers flock here from all over the world, hoping to leave their mark on this timeless medium.

Every globe produced at Bellerby & Co. requires several days of work.

The hand-painted strips of paper are hung out to dry while waiting to be applied.

Craftsmen make bases from different materials (particularly wood) on the first floor.

These strips are intended for an astronomical globe.

Peter Bellerby, the firm's founder, strikes a pose in his workshop.

Each strip is delicately positioned by hand on the surface of the globe.

The illustrations are individually painted in watercolors by the artists in the workshop.

Known as the "Winston Churchill", this globe is 50 inches (127 cm) in diameter and stands on an oak base.

Bellerby & Co. has brought the ancient art of globe-making back from the brink.

Camden
ERSKINE
ROAD
LEMONIA
THREE COURS
SET LUNCH
£19.50
MONDAY TO FRIDAY

ABOVE

The picturesque facades of the houses in Primrose Hill.

OPPOSITE

There's a village-like atmosphere on every street corner of this area.

ABOVE

There are plenty of celebrities living behind the elegant exteriors of Hampstead, an area much loved for its tranquility and green surroundings.

OPPOSITE

Whether elegant brick edifices, rural Victorian cottages, or the creations of a contemporary architect, the houses in Hampstead are often larger than in other areas of London.

WELL RD. NW.3.

DEEP DIVE

BRITISH CHEESE

British food may not always be widely known or appreciated, but it is in fact very rich, as the diversity of its cheeses clearly demonstrates, with more than 700 varieties listed throughout the country by the British Cheese Board. Some have achieved world fame while others are less well known, but they all deserve their place on the cheeseboard!

Cheddar or Stilton would generally be the first to spring to mind, but there is a long-standing tradition for regional cheese. With its green pastureland, the country produces "mainly *tomme*-style cheese from cow's milk and some washed-rind soft cheeses like the famous Stinking Bishop", explains Jake Chapman, a cheese expert at Provisions, a delicatessen in Islington and Hackney.

The art of cheesemaking was brought here by the Roman legions and developed in medieval monasteries. Production declined drastically due to rationing in the 1940s, but several parallel movements conspired to resurrect it thirty years later. As our cheese lover recounts: "For one thing, dairy producers were transforming their surpluses into classic British cheeses, the 'territorial' cheeses, and there were also hippies who had crisscrossed Europe who were experimenting with goat and sheep's cheeses, such as the pioneering Mary Holbrook in Somerset."

Unlike strictly regulated regional cheeses from areas of France, the legendary recipes and producers are part of a wider British cheese patrimony. "It is the beauty but also the tragedy of our industry," explains Jake.

There are now only eighteen varieties protected by a European appellation (i.e. about 2.5 percent!), and the legendary Berkswell has disappeared as its makers have retired. Tunworth, a local Camembert, has narrowly escaped the same fate.

All hope is not lost, however. Shorter supply chains have been on the rise since Brexit, and thanks to artisan cheesemakers and processors such as Neal's Yard Dairy, so-called territorial cheese such as Caerphilly, Wensleydale, Double Gloucester, and Lancashire are making a comeback. There is still a strong tradition of hard cheeses, however, with the unassailable Cheddar front and center and accounting for half of all national consumption. Stilton, a creamy blue cheese, is a fixture for special occasions. Some producers have even gone as far as recreating forgotten recipes such as Stichelton, the raw milk forerunner of Stilton. In 2023, 521,000 tonnes of cheese were produced in the United Kingdom, a figure that is constantly increasing, along with the number of producers. British cheese-making culture is "in constant flux" but has a bright future ahead of it.

A MAP OF CHEESEMAKING

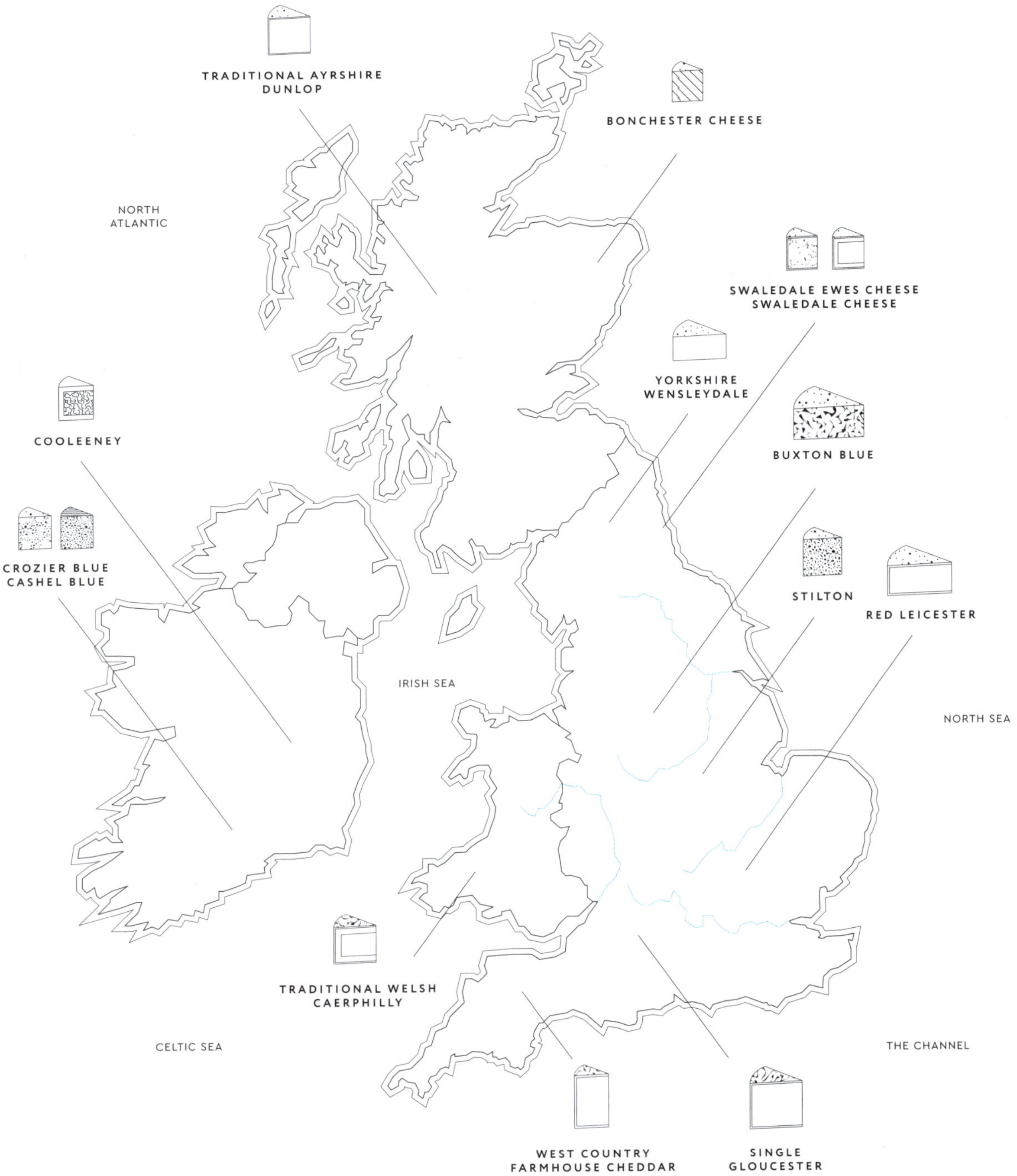

MADE IN UK

With so many cheeses being produced up and down the country, the United Kingdom can certainly look its European cousins in the eye.

ABOVE

The natural world features on the housefronts of wealthy Hampstead, such as this climbing passionflower.

OPPOSITE

Hampstead Heath is one of London's largest parks and a haven for local flora and fauna; it is a great place for a weekend stroll or a picnic.

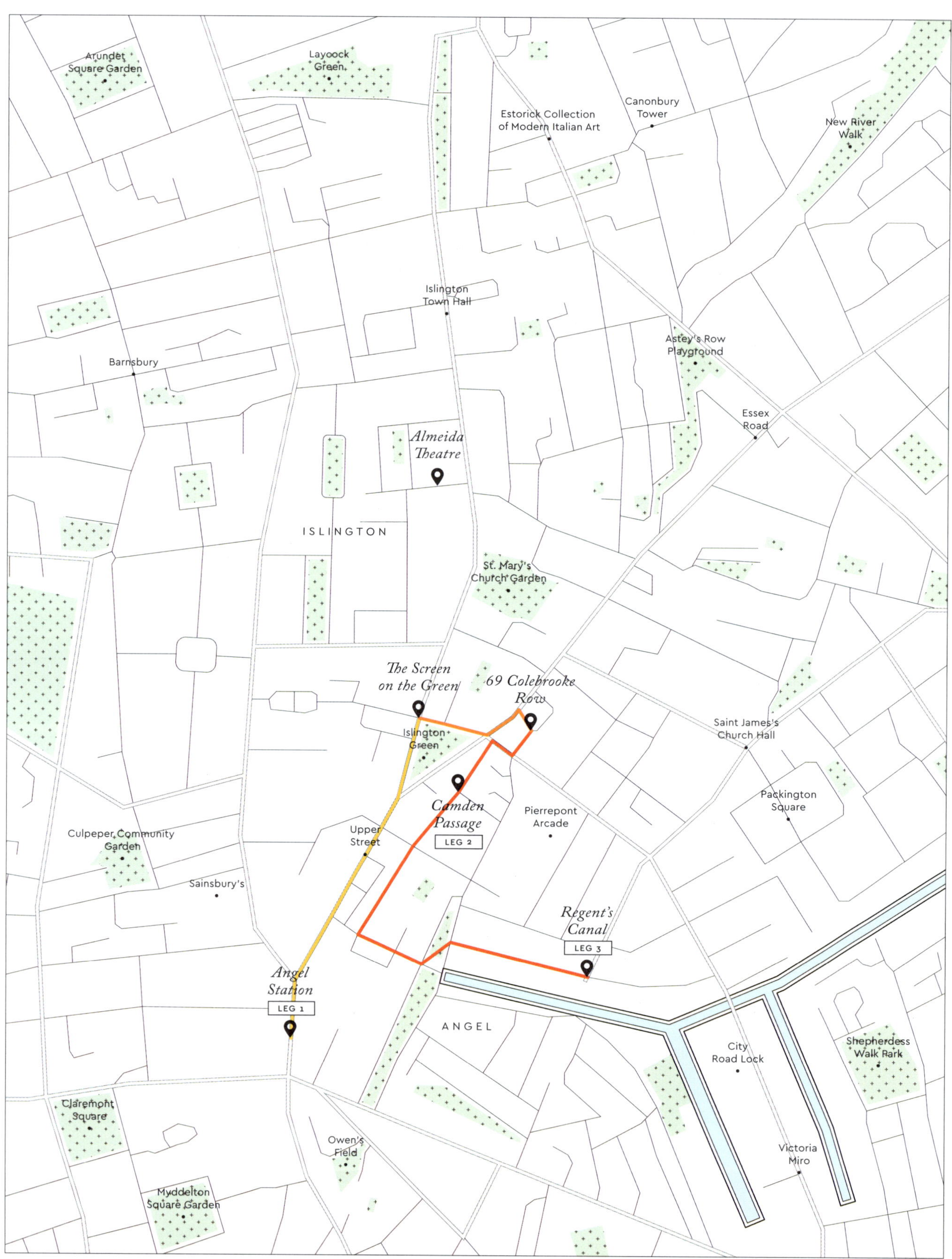
Arundel Square Garden
Layoock Green
Estorick Collection of Modern Italian Art
Canonbury Tower
New River Walk
Islington Town Hall
Barnsbury
Astey's Row Playground
Essex Road
Almeida Theatre
ISLINGTON
St. Mary's Church Garden
The Screen on the Green
69 Colebrooke Row
Islington Green
Saint James's Church Hall
Camden Passage
LEG 2
Pierrepont Arcade
Packington Square
Upper Street
Culpeper Community Garden
Sainsbury's
Regent's Canal
LEG 3
Angel Station
LEG 1
ANGEL
City Road Lock
Shepherdess Walk Park
Claremont Square
Owen's Field
Victoria Miro
Myddelton Square Garden

WALKING TOUR

ANGEL

Angel is a small gem in the borough of Islington; one of those neat areas of London where the living is easy, with cultural life, gastropubs, stylish boutiques, and a whiff of fresh air along the Regent's Canal. From Upper Street to the neighboring district of De Beauvoir Town in Hackney, it offers everything you could want or need.

LEG 1 : A BIT OF CULTURE

Get off the Tube at Angel (on the Northern Line) and head north along Upper Street to the fork in the road at Islington Green. The red neon of the Screen on the Green sign has been shining out over the main road since 1913. This Art Deco cinema with its preserved facade is one of the oldest still in operation in the country, and has retained its old-fashioned charm. Settle comfortably into one of the velvet seats in its only auditorium, order a cocktail directly from the bar at the back of the hall, and enjoy an arthouse movie or a blockbuster, depending on the day. Theater lovers should venture to the junction of Upper Street and Almeida Street to find a small venue with a challenging program of contemporary drama. The reputation of the Almeida theater has spread far beyond the local neighborhood.

LEG 2 : CAMDEN PASSAGE

Now head west across Islington Green and lose yourself in Camden Passage as the frenzy of the main road suddenly gives way to a narrow, cobbled lane. This charming pedestrianized area is a realm of antiques dealers, interior designers, small cafés, and the usual food shops; life moves at a different pace here. There is a flea market here twice a week (Wednesday and Saturday) to the delight of bargain hunters on the look-out for vinyl, vintage fashion, floral-patterned crockery, engraved crystal glassware, lamps, or old linen. Go in the morning and take the opportunity to explore the miniature shops along Pierrepont Arcade.

LEG 3 : REGENT'S CANAL WALK

Halfway down the passage, head east along Charlton Place toward Colebrooke Row, an elegant, garden-lined street of Georgian architecture. Number 69 discreetly comes to life in the evenings as it is home to a famous but cozy cocktail bar, but during the day continue on south and head down a small ramp to reach Regent's Canal Walk by the opening of the Islington tunnel. As soon as the sun makes an appearance, locals head to the the benches around City Road Lock to read or picnic to the merry honking of the ducks and swans. The banks of London's canals are the ideal place for a bucolic stroll. Continue on to the Towpath café, the best kept secret on a path lined with colorful canalboats (open March to November).

NECKINGER MILLS
BEVINGTONS & SONS

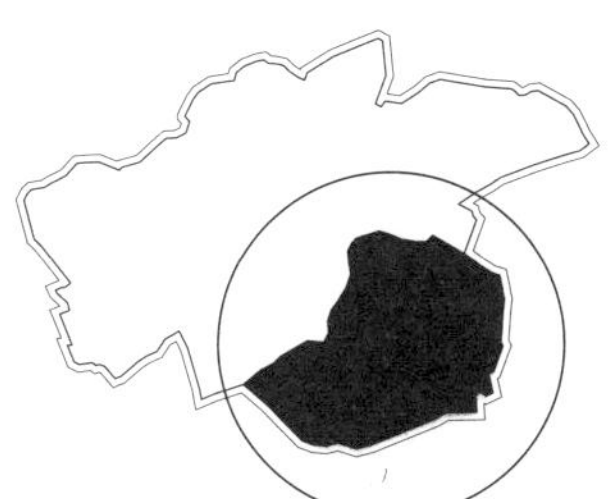

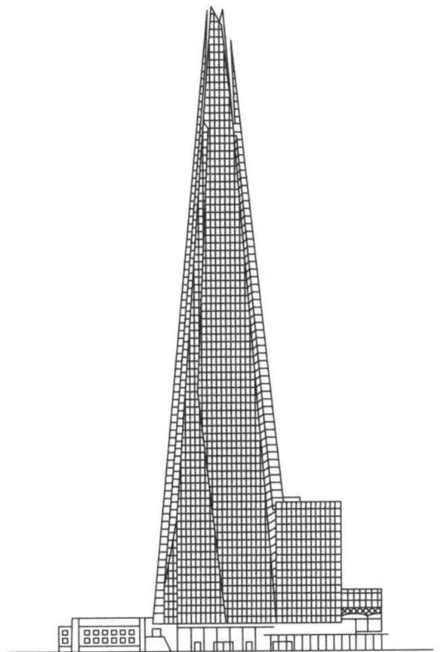

BERMONDSEY, BOROUGH, BRIXTON, VAUXHALL, PECKHAM

SOUTH

The industrial past, waves of immigration, and entertainment have all shaped the lively neighborhoods south of the Thames over the centuries. From Brixton to Peckham and Bermondsey, the boroughs of Southwark and Lambeth demonstrate the diversity and cultural wealth of the capital.

P.134

The old industrial Neckinger Mills, once owned by the Bevington family, were named after an underground watercourse that crosses Bermondsey. The facade is now listed.

OPPOSITE

There are lots of little lanes in the area around Bermondsey Street, like this one leading to Carmarthen Place.

Think of south London and Brixton often comes to mind as the multicultural reference point for this part of the city, despite the various tumultuous periods in its past. Brixton has been an urban suburb since the Industrial Revolution and became the home of the Afro-Caribbean community in the mid-19th century with the arrival of the migrants of the Windrush Generation. This district in the borough of Lambeth is also a musical hotspot and the heart of both the reggae and punk scenes, with legendary venues that include the Ritzy and Brixton Academy.

Historic Southwark along the Thames is the oldest borough. Bermondsey made a name for itself as an important religious and agricultural hub in the Middle Ages but the so-called granary of London was transformed in the Victorian era into an industrial area of tanneries, docks, and food industries. The 20th century has seen the district gentrify, and art galleries and famous bistros have moved into the old brick warehouses of Bermondsey, turning the area into a popular destination. At the weekend, head for the arcades of Maltby Street Market under the railway arches and dive fork-first into the city's array of culinary delights.

Vauxhall, to the west of Waterloo, has always been a destination for entertainment, and the shows and concerts of Vauxhall Gardens were the height of London's urban culture in the 17th and 18th centuries. The area is still popular with night owls for its LGBTQ+ clubs, and it is also home to the SIS Building, the headquarters of MI6, the British secret service made popular by the legendary Bond, James Bond.

The Victorian terraces and Georgian townhouses a little way to the southwest have made Clapham a very popular residential area for young families, and the green spaces of Clapham Common underline its village-like atmosphere in the middle of the city, while its many bars also attract young professionals.

Finally, Peckham to the southeast has become one of London's coolest creative hubs. Known as Little Lagos due to its large Nigerian community, this once working-class neighborhood has also housed a diverse and dynamic artistic crowd who have been gathering around local institutions such as the Bussey Building since the late 1990s. The bustling streets around Rye Lane are a good example of the area's multiculturalism, with a whiff of gentrification.

SOUTH

THE ESSENTIALS

49

BRIXTON VILLAGE

This covered arcade-style market in the heart of cosmopolitan Brixton is divided into two alleys, Market Row and Granville Arcade.

50

BERMONDSEY STREET

The main street in Bermondsey is resolutely hedonistic, alternating stylish restaurants, small cafés, museums, and art galleries.

51

BOROUGH MARKET

Borough Market is the oldest food market in the British capital and has officially been in operation since 1756.

52

BLACK CULTURAL ARCHIVES

This Brixton archive and heritage center has been dedicated to the country's Afro-Caribbean population since 1981.

53

BRIXTON O2 ACADEMY

This former Art Deco movie theater is a historic monument and has become a legendary gig venue in south London.

54

PECKHAM

Peckham in the southeast is a multi-faceted area of cultural and artistic interest.

55

ELEPHANT AND CASTLE

This area undergoing renewal is known for its nightlife and shopping mall, one of the first in the country in the 1960s.

56

YOUNG VIC

As the name suggest, this is the definitive stage on which to see the great artists of tomorrow perform.

57

WHITE CUBE

This contemporary art gallery founded by Jay Jopling in Bermondsey Street in 1993 has acquired an international reputation.

58

THE SHARD

Renzo Piano's skyscraper, with its luxury homes and a fancy hotel at the summit, opened in 2012.

59

OLD VIC

Productions in this theater founded to the southeast of Waterloo station in 1818 have achieved global renown.

60

RITZY CINEMA

This movie theater opened its doors in 1911 and is now a historic monument and a stalwart of the Brixton scene, with gigs and events held regularly upstairs.

ABOVE

Bermondsey Street delis are known for their aesthetic appeal and careful sourcing of produce.

OPPOSITE

More than a hundred shops and stalls in Borough Market are crammed with fresh produce and street food specialties from around the world.

FOOD AND DRINK

MALTBY STREET MARKET

A CULINARY MELTING-POT

This narrow lane topped with colorful flags transforms itself into a market every weekend, with international street food.

LONG TABLES

Before entering the Ropewalk, visitors can enjoy eating at the large picnic tables set up for the occasion.

SOMETHING FOR EVERYONE

Vietnamese *banh-mi* or a spicy Ethiopian stew? London's multicultural offerings have been displayed in the open-air market since 2010.

A LOCAL SPOT

Maltby Street Market is popular amongst London foodies who want to avoid the crowds in nearby Borough Market.

OPEN ALL HOURS

Delicatessens, craft brewers, and restaurants with shady terraces are open every day of the week.

OPEN-AIR LABORATORY

Many mainstream ventures began by trialing their recipes at this market.

LIVING THE GOOD LIFE

Spend a Saturday with a drink or two in the restaurants tucked away under the railway arches.

WORLD TOUR

Freshly garnished Greek *souvlaki*, homemade Argentine empanadas, or a piping hot British toastie: choosing is the hardest part.

ABOVE

Grange Road is a mix of recently renovated buildings and Porsches alternating with more modest homes.

OPPOSITE

Now transformed into apartments, the Barrow Hepburn & Gale Ltd factory was known for manufacturing the red leather ministerial boxes that are the symbols of constitutional monarchy.

ARTS AND CRAFTS

BLENHEIM FORGE

URBAN KNIFE-MAKING

In addition to use as storage space for a myriad of things, the arches of London's railways have housed shops and workshops since the 19th century. The many restaurants, boutiques, and workshops with a new breed of artisan are breathing new life into these spaces that are so typical of the urban landscape. This is certainly true of the three young men at Blenheim Forge, the definitive knifemakers who have settled in south London's Peckham Rye.

It all began in the nearby garden of engineer James Ross-Harris and philosophy Ph.D student Jon Warshawsky. As Sunday DIYers, the young housemates were looking for a new project, and with just a few disobliging bricks, a leaf blower, and some charcoal, the first carbon blades were soon taking shape on their makeshift forge. With a fascination for the positioning of steel in Japanese blades, they learnt on the job, helped on their way by a few vague videos and a lot of practice on scrap metal.

In 2014, the historic forge at Blenheim Grove in Peckham was looking for a buyer, and this was the spark; Richard Warner joined them on the adventure and Blenheim Forge officially opened its doors. The red wrought-iron gates of arch 229 is inconspicuous from the street, but beyond lie the definitive knives for fans of Japanese blades made in London.

The urban maker scene was flourishing at the time; "This booming local community was a true source of inspiration. Chatting with chefs, artists, artisans, and creative types over a pint at the pub played a key role in our success", James reveals. Enter through the gates and you will first encounter a shop with wall displays of the *santokus*, *gyotos*, *nakiris* and other multi-use blades of sophisticated design that have made their name. Their early creations have been framed in a corner as a reminder of the progress that has been made in a decade. There is a reverent silence in the workshop at the back of the shop.

Fifty pieces are produced here every month, along with a few very limited editions that offer an opportunity for each cofounder to express some individuality, often in collaboration with famous chefs or craftsmen. From hunting knives to meat cleavers to Damascus steel breadknives, their style will change according to the experience and wishes of each of these.

Forging by hand, heat treatment, honing; the trio are perfectionists and are in charge at every stage. Their blades combine the Rolls-Royce of Japanese carbon steel with their own blend of stainless steel and the delicate octagonal handles are sourced from local tree species that have fallen naturally in the royal parks. The cases are hand-stitched by local leatherworker Harry Owen. The ultimate luxury and an index of top-level craftsmanship is that you can come and have your knife sharpened free of charge at the workshop for life.

1/ JAMES ROSS-HARRIS

The co-founder of Blenheim Forge strikes a pose in his workshop.

2/ LOCAL RESOURCES

Walnut, chestnut, and English maple that has fallen naturally are given a second life.

3/ *SANTOKUS*

These *santoku* knives are waiting patiently on the bench for the back of their blades to be burnished.

4/ MACHINES

Professional machinery like this sand blaster is used for some of the many painstaking stages in knife-making.

5/ A HELPING HAND

Wet-sanding blades to sharpen them requires high precision work to give them a perfect edge.

ABOVE

The Senegalese flag is displayed proudly over this exotic grocery store in Granville Arcade, Brixton Village.

OPPOSITE

You can't miss the African, Caribbean, South American, and Asian stores on Electric Avenue in Brixton Market.

43
LONDON AFRO HALAL BUTCHER
GROCERY - FRUIT & VEG
LONDON AFRO HALAL BUTCHER
GROCERY - FRUIT & VEG

The wall of this house in Brixton's Windrush Square has been nicknamed the "Bovril Wall" for the advertisement that can still be seen there.

The contrast between the typical Victorian red-brick facades on Electric Avenue and the multiculturalism of its stores embodies the spirit of Brixton.

DEEP DIVE

GIN

The famous London dry gin, historic Plymouth gin with its protected recipe, sweet old tom gin, and sloe gin are just some of the many different options. There is not just one gin, but instead a multitude, with a variety of distillation processes and aromatic profiles. The spirit is almost as deeply rooted in British culture as tea, but it spent a long time out of favor before returning to Britain's good books at the turn of the 21st century.

Jenever, a malted spirit infused with juniper berries that was drunk for medical purposes, first appeared in the Netherlands, rather than the United Kingdom, in the 17th century. It reached the shores of England in 1688 thanks to the new monarch, William III, Prince of Orange and the son of Mary Henrietta Stuart.

A gin craze eventually seized the country in the 18th century, affecting the less privileged amongst the population in particular, and in just a few years, more than 6,000 gin parlors and 1,500 stills sprang up all over London. Annual production approached 12 million gallons (45 million liters), which equates to four double gins a day for every man, woman, and child! To put a stop to a public health problem that was slowly destroying the nation, the government passed a slew of Gin Acts in quick succession and the rot gut that was available for a few shillings disappeared in favor of a higher quality alcohol, leading to the advent of London dry gin, which was unsweetened and remains the world's bestseller to this day. The sweeter old tom gin was very popular at the time, and in this way gin began its slow social ascent.

British colonists in 19th-century India were obliged to drink tonic water containing quinine to combat malaria, and, combining business with pleasure, they added their favorite spirits and the G&T (gin-and-tonic) was born. By the 2000s, it was the turn of the craft movement and a renewal of interest in cocktails to revolutionize gin culture and artisan distilleries flourished, often favoring limited edition batches with local and organic ingredients. It was much the same story with tonics, the selection and pairing of which also became important for revealing new aromatic complexities. A leading figure in this renaissance was the artisanal Sipsmith distillery, which opened its doors in 2009 after successfully appealing the law of 1823 that prohibited the granting of licenses for small-quantity distilling. With more than a thousand (and rising) distilleries across the United Kingdom, producers are vying in inventiveness to carve out a niche for themselves, and gin (with or without alcohol) is in ever greater demand. To appreciate its fantastic diversity, visit the capital's specialist bars, which may stock up to 500 varieties.

PRODUCING RECTIFIED SPIRIT

A

B

C

D

01

PREPARING THE BOTANICALS

A Juniper B Angelica C Cardamom D Coriander

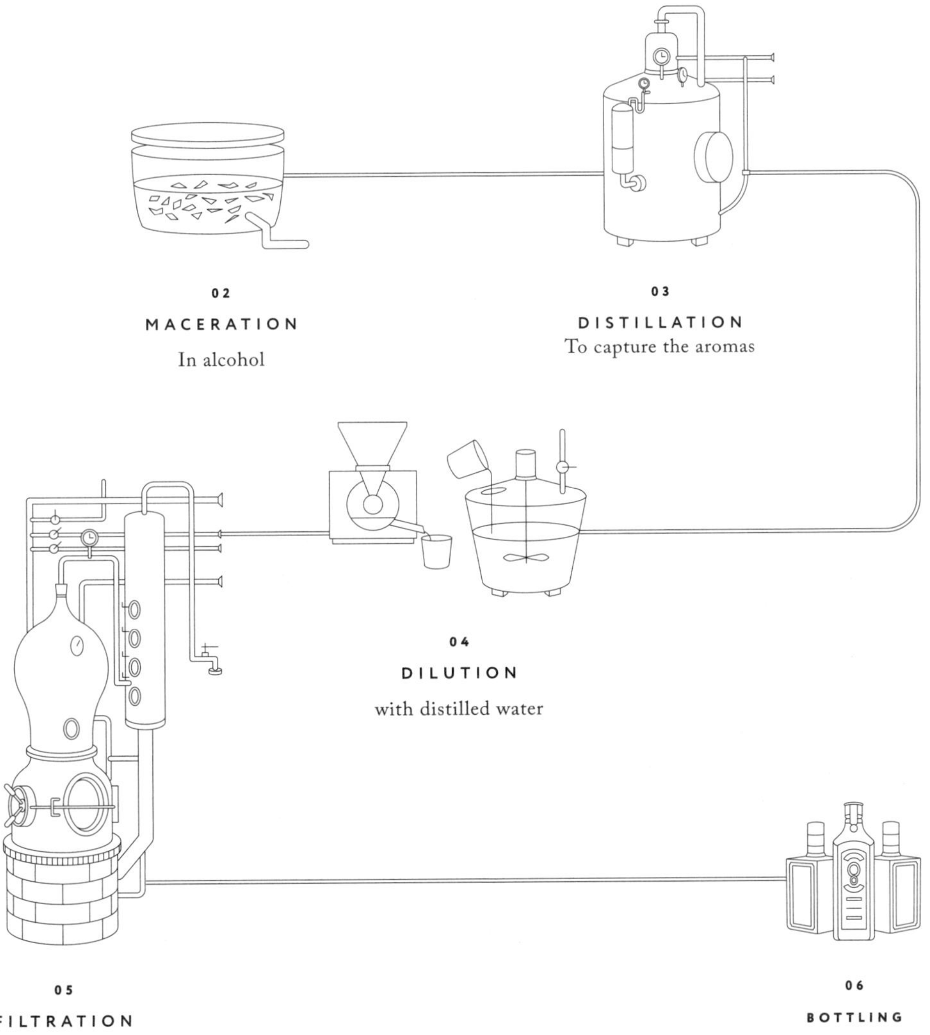

02

MACERATION

In alcohol

03

DISTILLATION

To capture the aromas

04

DILUTION

with distilled water

05

FILTRATION

Or clarity and purity

06

BOTTLING

Bermondsey's industrial past can still be glimpsed on every street, in its dilapidated storefronts like this green-tiled specimen in Long Lane, for example.

D RUG CO.
74
74
74

ABOVE

This building topped with three feathers representing the Prince of Wales (along with his motto, "Ich dien") can be seen at the bustling crossroads of Brixton Junction.

OPPOSITE

This red-brick building dating from 1908 is the headquarters of the borough of Lambeth, and is known as Brixton Town Hall.

LAMBETH TOWN HALL
Brixton 109
arriva

BERMONDSEY SQUARE
Nº3

ABOVE

Sculptures on the facade of the former London Leather, Hide and Wool Exchange recount the various stages of leatherworking.

OPPOSITE

Bermondsey Square is known for its antiques market and a wide variety of cultural events.

HISTORY

THE TANNERIES OF BERMONDSEY

Bermondsey is now a trendy area of southeast London, but it has a rich tradition of leatherworking, and the history of its tanneries can still be read in the exteriors of the factories and warehouses of this reborn cultural and culinary hub.

The first tanneries date back to the 16th century and these were concentrated a fair way from the center on the far bank of the Thames because of the strong smells they generated. Queen Anne granted Bermondsey's guild of tanners a royal charter in 1703, formalizing a long-standing local tradition of craftsmanship. The tanning business flourished in the 18th century as water resources were guaranteed by the tides that flowed rhythmically up the river. The area was known as Leather Market and became an important industrial hub as the tanneries attracted workers from all over the country to meet growing demand for shoes, belts, and bags. Prominent people were major players in the local economy and invested in the life of the area, including Samuel Bevington, a member of a respected family who became the first mayor of the brand-new borough of Bermondsey in 1900. His statue is still to be found looking out over Tooley Street.

The big names in the industry teamed up in 1870 to create their own market for hides – the London Leather, Hide and Wool Exchange. This building still stands proudly on the corner of Weston Street and Leathermarket Street; around fifty tanners, skinners, and curriers (specialists in the treatment and preparation of leather) would have worked under the same roof here. The medallion bas-reliefs decorating the facade have been preserved and depict the stages of leatherworking from initial treatment to final inspection.

Bermondsey's tanneries were slowly overtaken by technological, regulatory, and environmental developments, however, and by the 20th century, a decline in operations was being accompanied by the urban renewal of the area, which opened the door for creative types looking for affordable premises to move in.

Bermondsey is now better known for its art galleries, fashionable restaurants, and sleek apartments built into the old brick warehouses, but its heritage is visible at every turn, from the placenames to the ghostly signs that still adorn the buildings.

This gateway on Grange Road leads to an Art Deco warehouse called the Alaska Building.

Tanner Street was named in 1881 in homage to the area's key activity.

The statue of Samuel Bevington is a tribute to his devotion to the area.

This apartment block has incorporated modern elements into the structure of the original tannery.

The London Leather, Hide and Wool Exchange was designed by George Elkington in 1870.

Twelve loft apartments have been built in this former Victorian spice warehouse.

This cozy pub sign in Long Lane harks back to the history of the area.

Pulleys and winches were once used to load and unload merchandise.

Bevingtons & Sons excelled in tanning leather for millinery and glove-making.

ABOVE

The facade of the warehouse once belonging to the famous Baylis & Co. Ltd tannery can still be seen on Morocco Street.

OPPOSITE

The Morocco Store in Bermondsey is an excellent example of a warehouse that has been carefully renovated to make elegant homes.

7-12
Apartments 7 - 12

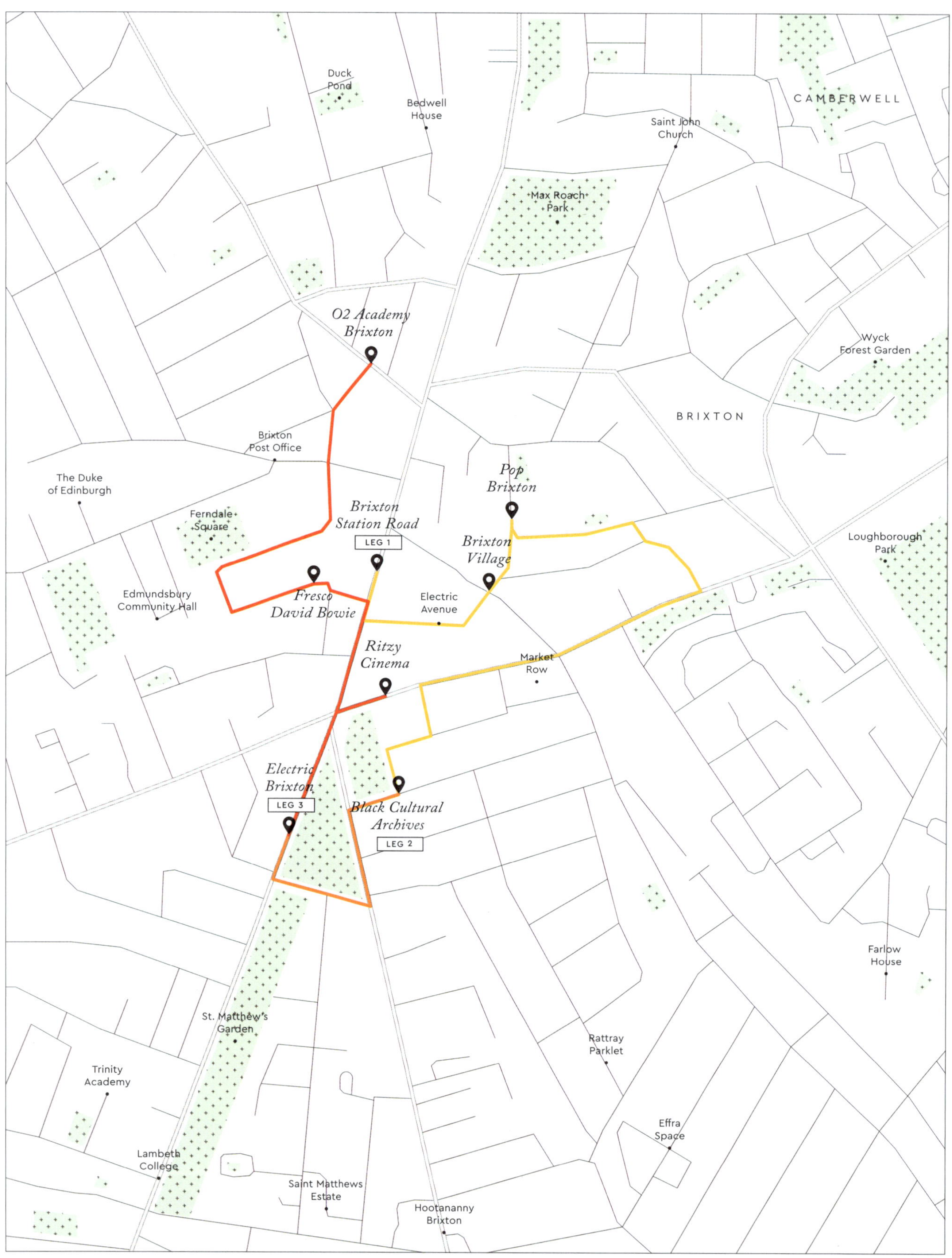

Duck Pond
Bedwell House
Saint John Church
CAMBERWELL
Max Roach Park
O2 Academy Brixton
Wyck Forest Garden
BRIXTON
Brixton Post Office
The Duke of Edinburgh
Pop Brixton
Brixton Station Road
LEG 1
Ferndale Square
Brixton Village
Loughborough Park
Edmundsbury Community Hall
Fresco David Bowie
Electric Avenue
Ritzy Cinema
Market Row
Electric Brixton
LEG 3
Black Cultural Archives
LEG 2
Farlow House
St. Matthew's Garden
Rattray Parklet
Trinity Academy
Effra Space
Lambeth College
Saint Matthews Estate
Hootananny Brixton

WALKING TOUR

BRIXTON

Lying at the southern end of the Victoria Line, Brixton has a unique energy, although for a time the area was unfortunately better known for the riots that shook it in 1981. Its rebellious and multicultural spirit has always made it a creative hub, especially in music, so enjoy this guided tour to the sound of the reggae that is regularly audible from many of its bustling street corners.

LEG 1 : THE MARKETS OF BRIXTON

In order to completely immerse yourself in the area's eclectic nature, head to the vibrant markets of Brixton. The open-air stalls on Electric Avenue and Brixton Station Road are crammed with fresh produce and international products. Brixton Village is made up of Market Row and the Granville Arcade. Under the glass roof of this former covered market built in the 1930s, you will find a collection of stalls selling Jamaican jerk chicken, *okonomiyaki* from Osaka, African textiles, and vintage fashion, as well as an inclusive bookshop, a Sierra Leonean grocer's, some contemporary art galleries, and a couple of trendy wine bars and coffee shops to boot. For a slightly more hipster take and a look at the changes taking place in south London, head for the Pop Brixton creative market, where the street food stands and urban craft pop-ups in shipping containers are made even livelier with regular events. Enjoy a stroll through this multicultural area.

LEG 2 : BLACK CULTURAL ARCHIVES

This museum, exhibition space, and cultural hub housed in a Georgian building on Windrush Square opened its doors in 1981 with a mission to celebrate the UK's Afro-Caribbean community through exhibitions, debate, and events. Its archived records are a living memory of stories that have often been overlooked in British history, from combatants in World War II to the Windrush generation, whose name is derived from the liner HMT *Empire Windrush*, from which many immigrants from Jamaica and Trinidad and Tobago disembarked at Tilbury during the 1950s. This destination is essential to an understanding of the richness and complexity of the history of Brixton, which is intimately entwined with the history of this community.

LEG 3 : MUSICAL

It's impossible to talk about Brixton without mentioning the key role it has played in the emergence of new musical talent. This fountainhead of reggae and ska in the 1970s and 1980s was also the place where David Bowie grew up (and you will find a fresco in his honor by the Australian artist Jimmy C at the entrance to Tunstall Road). The area is crammed with several iconic concert halls and clubs, including Electric Brixton, Upstairs at the Ritzy, and the Windmill, while the O2 Brixton Academy has hosted the cream of British artists beneath its cupola, with locals such as David Bowie, Adele, The Clash, Radiohead, and Florence and the Machine lighting up the stage of this listed former Art Deco movie theater.

Congestion charging zone
C
Mon - Fri
7am - 6pm
Sat, Sun &
Bank hol
Noon - 6pm
½ mile ahead
RED ROUTE
PBS
Traffic enforcement cameras
ROAD AHEAD CLOSED
Wood Green 243

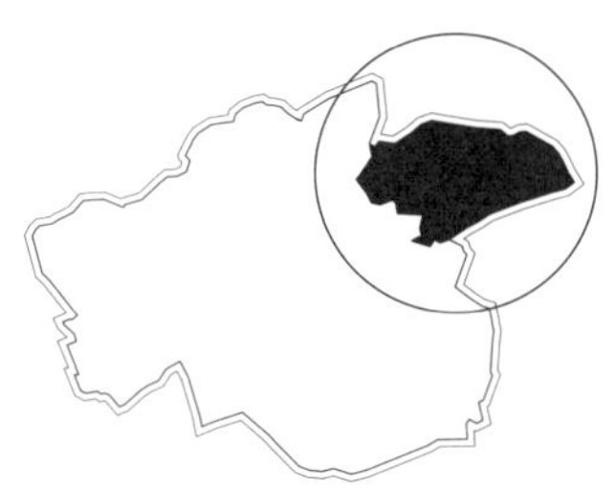

BETHNAL GREEN, EAST END, HACKNEY, SHOREDITCH, WHITECHAPEL

EAST

East London is a place of stark contrasts. It is both one of the most deprived and the most gentrified areas of the capital, as social housing, Victorian terraces, and modern apartments jostle for space with old warehouses, the last witnesses of its industrial past and now transformed into residential complexes. This resolutely cosmopolitan area has been shaped by waves of immigration and is home to a mixture of long-standing residents, artists, and employees from the creative and technology industries who are looking for something a bit different.

P.166

Shoreditch, to the north of the Square Mile, extends along both sides of Shoreditch High Street and has become a byword for the gentrification of East London.

OPPOSITE

The Palm Tree, built in 1666, is a last remnant of a street swept away by the Blitz, and you can still pop in for a drink in this pub in Mile End Park.

The area of East London straddling the boroughs of Tower Hamlets and Hackney also has a long tradition of welcoming newcomers, from French Huguenots to Orthodox Jewish communities and the Pakistani diaspora. More than eighty-nine languages are thought to be spoken here. It is also a young and dynamic part of the capital, with half the residents aged under thirty-five.

London's contemporary art scene began to take off in these formerly industrial areas in the 1980s. Propelled by artists like Damien Hirst and Tracey Emin, Shoreditch, Dalston, and Bethnal Green would become the focal point of alternative cultural activity. There is still a hint of this spirit, even if things have sometimes appeared a little more sedate since the City yuppies and the start-up mob have taken up residence here. This evolution is most obvious in Shoreditch, where thoroughfares like Redchurch Street seem to have been taken over by coffee shops, fashion labels, boutique hotels, and trendy restaurants. The area around Old Street, on the border with Islington, is known as Silicon Roundabout and Tech City due to the concentration of tech companies located in its immediate surroundings.

Running between Shoreditch and Whitechapel, Brick Lane remains an icon of the rough-and-ready spirit of the East End, while also being popular with tourists visiting this open-air gallery street during the weekend. Murals by street artists like Banksy and Stik look down on vintage clothes sold by weight, secondhand dealers, and curry houses that bear witness to the strong Bangladeshi community. The picturesque cobblestones of Columbia Road, lined with little independent boutiques, are emblematic of the neighborhood's rebellious spirit. The stalls of its Sunday morning flower market can be particularly busy.

The area around the main commercial strip of Mare Street, to the north, has seen co-working spaces, bike shops, and bars replace the weavers, rag trade workshops, and other warehouses abandoned in its post-industrial decline. The ultimate charm of the area is in the breath of fresh air offered by the towpath along the Regent's Canal and the 213 acres (86 ha) of Victoria Park, with its lake and pagoda, both classic destinations for locals venturing out on a weekend stroll.

THE
PALM
TREE
THE PALM TREE

THE ESSENTIALS

61

MUSEUM OF THE HOME

This Hoxton museum, housed in former almshouses, explores British interiors from 1600 to the present day.

62

BRICK LANE

This cosmopolitan East London street, popular with tourists, is known for its street food markets, Bangladeshi curry houses, and street art.

63

BROADWAY MARKET

This London street lined with small boutiques and restaurants is brought to life every weekend by a market that is typical of the spirit of the area.

64

YOUNG V&A

This branch of the renowned V&A is located in Bethnal Green and is dedicated to design for children. It has been completely renovated.

65

REGENT'S CANAL

The towpath along the eastern stretch of the Regent's Canal linking Paddington and Limehouse is a perfect place for a stroll.

66

ROUGH TRADE EAST

The flagship outlet of this musical institution is located in the cultural space of the Old Truman Brewery, near Brick Lane, and is a popular destination for fans of vinyl and live music.

67

LONDON FIELDS

Redesigned along its northern and eastern borders after bombing during the Blitz, the park is now a popular relaxation spot with local residents.

68

TEA BUILDING

The 1930s edifice in Shoreditch was once a Lipton's tea warehouse but now houses a host of stylish businesses, including Michelin-starred restaurants, members' clubs for the creative industries, studios and even a swimming pool on its roof terrace.

69

SHOREDITCH

The walls of Shoreditch are a magnet for street art and are decorated with graffiti by artists like Banksy and Ben Eine.

70

COLUMBIA ROAD FLOWER MARKET

Come on Sunday, at first light, for the most Instagrammed flower market in the capital.

71

WHITECHAPEL GALLERY

This renowned contemporary art gallery in the heart of the East End opened in 1901.

72

VICTORIA PARK

"Vicky Park" is the largest park in Tower Hamlets and opened its gates to the public in 1845. The area's green lung is 213 acres (86 ha) in size.

ABOVE

Towpath, a seasonal café on the canal near De Beauvoir Town, is a delight for its regulars as they stroll beside the water between March and November.

OPPOSITE

The back gardens of these typical brick terraces are right next to the canal and its vegetation.

ART

CAMILLE WALALA

DRESSING UP THE CITY

Camille Walala, a French artist who has been based in Hackney for more than twenty-five years, insinuates her joyful, daring, and playful artwork into the landscape of London and beyond.

“Walala” is a nod both to French pronunciation and to the communicative energy of Camille Vic-Dupont, and her artist’s name, inherited from her first email address, fits her like a glove. After arriving in London in 1997, the then twenty-three-year-old from Provence was instantly captivated by “this freedom to be entirely yourself. And I’ve never left since!” she says with a laugh.

Five years later, she discovered screen printing and went back to school to pursue a course option in textile design. Her graphic reproductions were brought to life on cushions that she initially sold at Broadway Market, but in 2012, the owner of Xoyo in Shoreditch gave her carte blanche to give the nightclub a new look. Camille thought big and finally found her inspiration to “use patterns and colors to create spaces where people feel good.”

It was her mural *Dream Come True* that propelled her to the top in 2010, however. Missing the sun of her native South of France, the wall painter brought “color into the gray” of Old Street, and the design’s instantly recognizable, hypnotically graphic shapes mix bright colors and deep black that melt into the city. She draws inspiration from all kinds of sources, including the Memphis Group, African prints, Vasarely, architectural details from her life in London, and much more.

“I also love the human aspect of the houses and the surrounding greenery, this village-like side in the heart of the city”, she confides. She has also set up her new studio a stone’s throw from Broadway Market and it has been decorated entirely in her own style, with a breathtaking view of the City. It is here she creates her colorful projects with a select team.

Through sheer tenacity, she slowly carved out a niche for herself in this urban space and in the spirit of London before extending her horizons. Canal boats, cars, pedestrian crossings, public transit stations, from New York to Hong Kong to Villeurbanne, the artist has transformed buildings and public spaces around the globe into true works of art. In Leyton, an eastern area of Greater London, the residents themselves asked her to reinvigorate their run-down high street. Now known as Walala Parade, it is the apple of the residents’ eye and Camille was delighted to brighten up their daily lives.

Camille is now exploring different media of artistic expression, including abstract painting – a world away from her signature straight lines, ceramics, and craftwork. It is all on a reduced scale, but new creative parameters are revealing themselves. Watch this space!

1/ CAMILLE WALALA

The artist at her desk in her studio near Broadway Market.

2/ MEMPHIS

This bookshelf designed by Ettore Sottsass is a Memphis Group icon and stands in pride of place in the studio.

3/ MIX & MATCH

The interior design of Camille Walala's studio matches her style.

4/ EXQUISITE SKETCHES

The patterns come first, then the colors.

ABOVE

The cobblestones, brick facades, and street art of Ezra Street, behind Columbia Road, all embody this small corner of London.

OPPOSITE

Broadway Market is lined with well-stocked boutiques, such as this famous bookstore.

6
THE BROADWAY BOOKSHOP

ABOVE

Ducks, swans, geese, and herons can be seen, and fed, in Victoria Park.

OPPOSITE

Rent a boat or a pedalo and explore the lake.

INTERIORS

HOUSE OF HACKNEY

FLOWER POWER

Taking inspiration from the natural world and from British craftsmanship, the House of Hackney label creates more than just interior design. Started in 2011, Frieda Gormley and Javvy M. Royle's brand has established a sustainable and responsible business model that harks back to the Arts and Crafts movement.

The House of Hackney was born from a desire "to bring our muse, Mother Nature, back into every home", recalls Frieda Gormley. First taking shape around their kitchen table in Hackney, their vision was at odds with the minimalism of the time. "After a decade of white walls, we dearly needed to surround ourselves with prints, colors, and textures", adds the firm's cofounder.

Bringing beauty to the people was one of the core principles of the Arts and Crafts movement that left a lasting mark on the landscape of British decorative arts. The members of this artistic movement, which started in the 19th century, promoted a return to craftsmanship and making things by hand, with respect for the human and the natural world. An iconic figure in the group was the committed artisan William Morris, "one of [our] heroes", who believed in art's ability to transform society. In developing iconic prints such as the Hollyhocks collection, House of Hackney have been preserving this heritage while infusing it with modern, occasionally even punky, touches. The couple sum up this philosophy as "buy less but better" as they strive to produce "future heirlooms" to be handed down and cherished for years to come.

The brand has put down solid roots, with showrooms in Shoreditch, Cornwall, and New York, along with a network of distributors round the globe. With their wallpaper, upholstery, furniture, lighting, and tableware, their naturalistic and colorful creations continue to point the way toward interior design that is different, daring, and committed. Their exuberant and fertile imaginations take inspiration from the work of visionaries "who set new standards of beauty" such as decorator Dorothy Draper, designer Elsie de Wolfe, singer David Bowie, and fashion designer Vivienne Westwood.

In their collections, Frieda Gormley and Javvy M. Royle uphold an ethical and aesthetic business model and make products locally using British craftspeople, echoing the ideals of the Arts and Crafts movement. With its powerful social and environmental vision, however, House of Hackney has gone beyond the merely aesthetic, and the brand has evolved over the years to incorporate principles of sustainability and regeneration. "The world doesn't need a new decor brand, it needs new meaning." In 2023 this dedication culminated in the appointment of Mother Nature and Future Generations to its board of directors, to give them a voice; as Frieda Gormley concludes, "We can't take without giving back".

MAXIMALISM

Prints and muted colors mingle and interact constantly, creating new harmonies.

BOTANICALS

Flora and fauna are brought to life by the attention to detail in the wallpapers, drapes, couches, and other textiles designed by the House of Hackney.

Brick Lane
London
EAST

ABOVE

Whitechapel has been multicultural for centuries and is considered the area most typical of the East End.

OPPOSITE

The Whitechapel Gallery is just round the corner from the exit of Aldgate East station.

DEEP DIVE

LIFE ON THE REGENT'S CANAL

With birds, city gardens, and narrowboats gliding along the water, it is difficult to believe you're still in London as you explore the tranquil walks along the Regent's Canal, which traverses the city from west to east.

The Regent's Canal is 9 miles (just over 14 km) long and crosses the capital from Paddington Basin in the west to Limehouse Basin in the east. It was designed to link the Grand Junction Canal to the Thames at the turn of the 19th century and named in honor of the Prince Regent (the future King George IV), and its waterways linked the city's various industrial hubs.

Construction was carried out under the leadership of architect John Nash and engineer James Morgan between 1812 and 1820. The first stretch, between Paddington and Camden Town, opened in 1816, while the second, which continued on to Regent's Canal Dock (now known as Limehouse Basin), the place where goods were transferred from cargo ships to canal boats, was completed in 1820.

This waterway was truly one of the city's industrial arteries and played an essential role in transporting coal, wood, iron, silver, cereals, leather, and even cheese. Competition from the railways gradually reduced traffic and caused it to fall into disuse before being completely abandoned until the mid-20th century. It was saved from oblivion at the end of the last century and now delights Londoners in search of tranquil surroundings a world away from the hectic bustle of their daily lives. This unexpected natural enclave is a paradise for ducks, swans, coots, moorhens, and kingfishers. The towpath was designed for horses to pull barges, but is now so crowded with cyclists, Sunday joggers, and strollers to the extent that in good weather it is a victim of its own success!

The old warehouses lining its banks are a testament to a not-so-distant past, and many of them have now been converted into coffee shops, artist studios, co-working spaces, galleries, and small boutiques, especially around Hackney. The narrowboats no longer transport goods but are an essential part of the local waterborne landscape. These typically slender craft are now home to a very close-knit, semi-nomadic community that lives according to the peaceful rhythm of the canal. Some have been turned into bookshops or floating restaurants, and you can charter one for a day's journey through the canal's twelve locks. This is yet another example of London's capacity for reinventing its industrial past as contemporary living space.

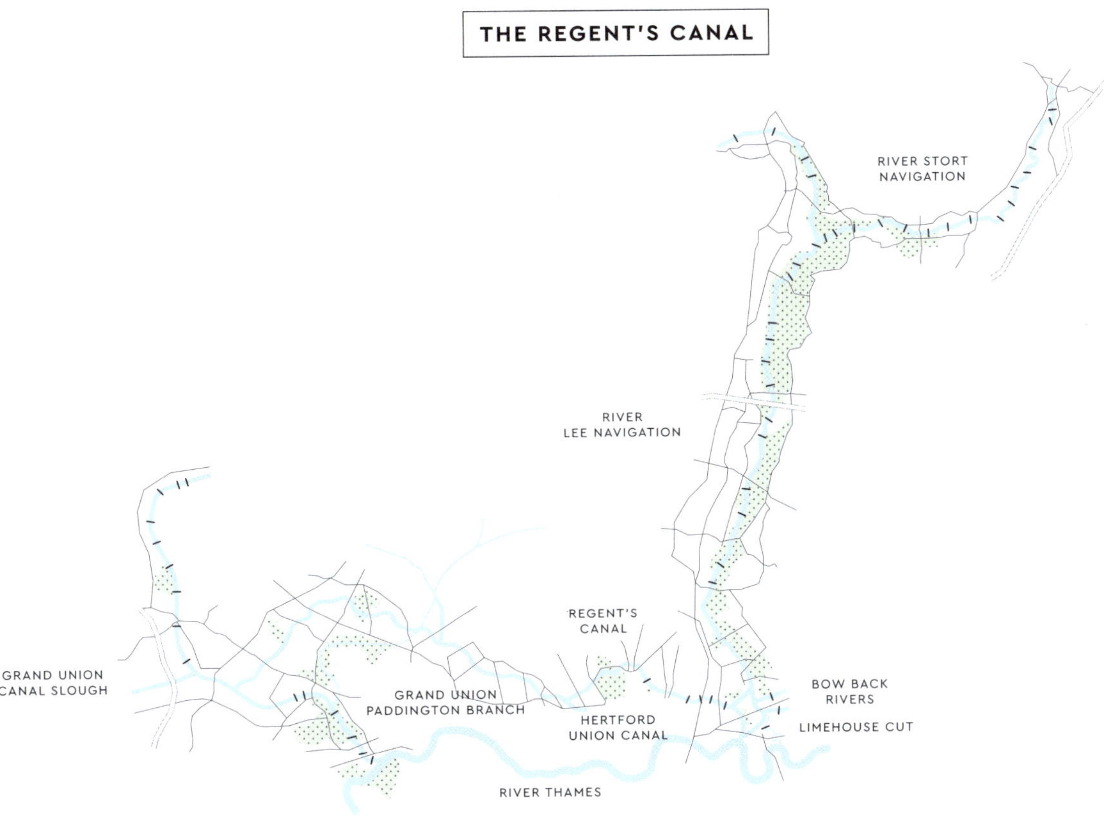

IN MOTION

Without a permanent mooring, narrowboats must move on every fortnight, a real life on the waves.

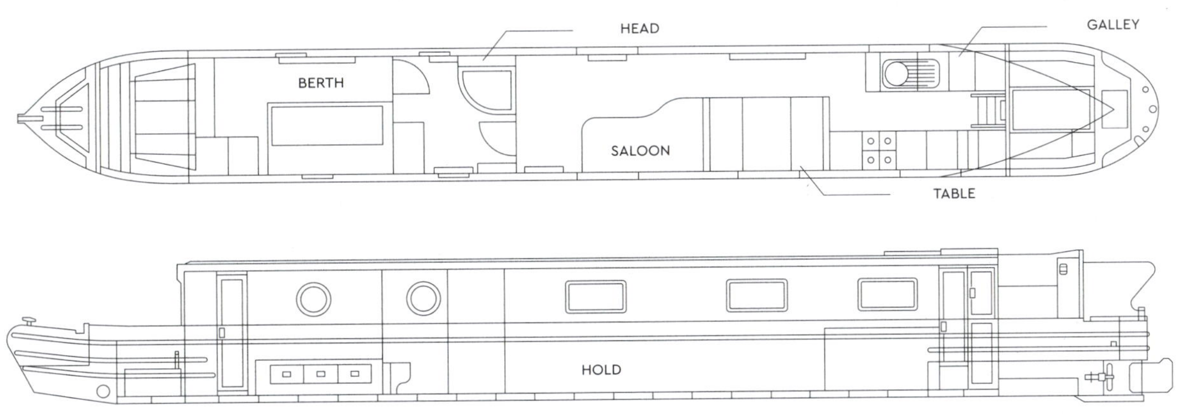

LAYOUT OF A NARROWBOAT

As the name might suggest, narrowboats are not wide and must be less than 7 feet (2.13 m) across to be able to navigate on British canals.

441
CES
739 8332

ABOVE

Painted doors and shutters bring a splash of color to Cyprus Street, near Bethnal Green.

OPPOSITE

With a pint of ale or a cocktail in hand, locals gather round the worn bar of this 1850s pub on Bethnal Green Road.

NATURE

LONDON FAUNA

AT LARGE

More than 600 deer run free in Richmond Park, London's biggest park.

SWANS

The swans of the Thames are counted in a ceremony known as "swan upping" in July.

HORSES

The Royal Horse Guards are part of the Household Cavalry.

SQUIRRELS

Spot squirrels in St James's Park.

DEER

Harts and does are one of the major attractions in Richmond Park.

SEAGULLS

The cries of seagulls are a constant companion in London life, especially in the morning.

FOXES

It is not unusual to encounter wild foxes on the street in London, which is home to almost 10,000 of them.

PARAKEETS

Bright green parakeets are ubiquitous in London's parks.

GRAY GEESE

The geese are not shy and will come to beg for crumbs.

STAGS

The antlers of this stag begin to grow in in spring and are cast in winter. They can grow by up to an inch (2.5 cm) each day.

ABOVE

This Victorian house on Shipton Street has been tastefully restored, retaining period architectural features such as the sash windows.

OPPOSITE

The reputation of this flower market has been attracting crowds to Columbia Road every Sunday since 1869.

FRENCH LAVENDER 3 for £10

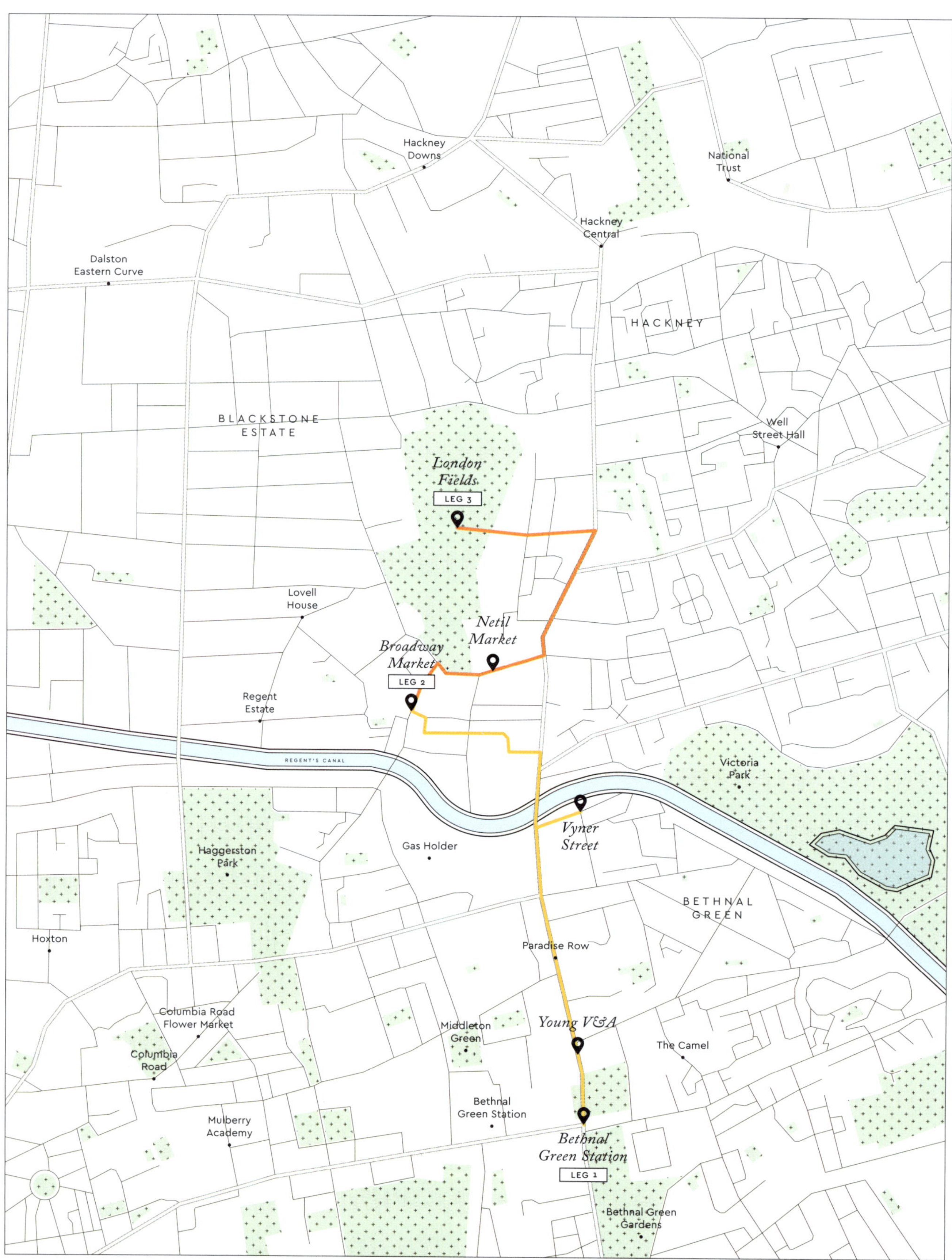
Hackney Downs
National Trust
Hackney Central
Dalston Eastern Curve
HACKNEY
BLACKSTONE ESTATE
Well Street Hall
London Fields
LEG 3
Lovell House
Netil Market
Broadway Market
LEG 2
Regent Estate
REGENT'S CANAL
Victoria Park
Vyner Street
Gas Holder
Haggerston Park
BETHNAL GREEN
Hoxton
Paradise Row
Columbia Road Flower Market
Middleton Green
Young V&A
The Camel
Columbia Road
Bethnal Green Station
Mulberry Academy
Bethnal Green Station
LEG 1
Bethnal Green Gardens

WALKING TOUR

FROM BETHNAL GREEN TO BROADWAY MARKET

To get a true sense of the transformation that East London has undergone since the 1980s, take a stroll from the railway arches of Bethnal Green to the greenery of London Fields, taking in the leafy banks of the Regent's Canal on the way. In this diverse area the last traces of an industrial past live alongside a rich artistic and creative scene.

LEG 1 : FROM BETHNAL GREEN TO THE REGENT'S CANAL

The diversity of the area strikes you as soon as you exit the Tube (the station was once an air-raid shelter and suffered a catastrophic crush in 1943). Head west along Roman Road toward Cambridge Heath. The Young V&A on the right, dedicated to childhood, is a subsidiary of the museum in South Kensington and is worth a visit. The arches of Paradise Row to the left are crammed with indie restaurants and bike shops. Before entering the Regent's Canal, take a moment to get lost in charming Vyner Street to the right, the heart of the East End art scene until the 2010s.

Take a left to enter the towpath along the canal. On the left you will see the latticework of Victorian gasometers, industrial symbols soon to become the luxury apartments of Broadway East and an example of the upmarket renovation that is transforming the neighborhood little by little every day.

LEG 2 : BROADWAY MARKET AND NETIL MARKET

Leave the peace and quiet of the canal and move on to Broadway Market, where the encounter between the traditional working classes and hipster modernity is in full swing, especially at number 9. Here you will still find the superb green and gold shopfront of F. Cooke's famous pie and mash shop, although a fashionable optician has replaced the Cockney institution of 1900. Take a look at the listed interior with its butter-yellow and turquoise tiling, now filled with tortoiseshell spectacle frames instead of jellied eels and pies. The surrounding area is a blend of bookmakers and liquor stores vying with artisan bakeries, arty bookshops, and fashionable bistros. The street is brought to life every weekend when a collection of street food stalls set up shop, representing the culinary variety of this highly diverse neighborhood.

Down to the right, heading toward Netil Market, you will find an old factory that has been converted into a creative hub. Somewhat more avant-garde than its neighbor, its courtyard comes alive at the end of the week, driven by projects from young chefs and artisans who often turn up to test out their ideas in its tiny outlets before making bigger plans. Don't miss the panoramic views of Hackney's ever-changing skyline from the rooftop.

LEG 3 : LONDON FIELDS

Sheep Lane and Lamb Lane are reminders of its pastoral past. London Fields has been a public space since the 16th century, with local residents and workers making full use of its 31 acres (12.65 ha) and amenities, including a cricket pitch and tennis courts, not to mention the famous Art Deco lido, with its 164-ft (50-m) heated swimming pool and café.

London Fields is the green lung of the area, especially since its redevelopment in 2013, and reflects the diversity of East London. Hipsters on fixed-wheel bikes and long-standing residents gather at the weekend for impromptu picnics, disposable barbecues, and a game of football. You're also more than likely to see coffee cups and punnets from the "chippy", the affectionate nickname for the fish and chip shop next door!

12

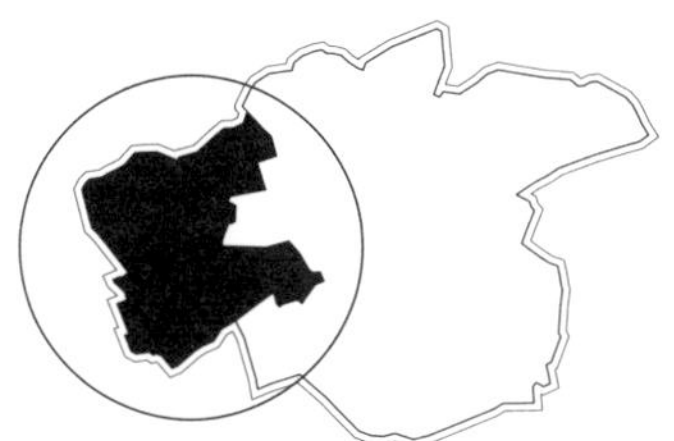

BELGRAVIA, HOLLAND PARK, KENSINGTON, KNIGHTSBRIDGE, NOTTING HILL, SOUTH KENSINGTON

WEST

Kensington, Chelsea, Knightsbridge, Belgravia, and Notting Hill are amongst the most exclusive and opulent areas of the capital. With their blend of splendid architecture, vast green spaces, prestigious museums, and luxury shopping, they attract a cosmopolitan population of celebrities and expatriates who are keen to discover a sophisticated London where life can be lived to the full.

P.194

Luxurious homes lurk behind the neat facades of Petersham Place, a charming cobbled mews in South Kensington.

OPPOSITE

The Royal Albert Hall in South Kensington features an iconic dome designed by Rowland Mason Ordish.

Kensington, the historic haunt of the social elite, owes its rise in fortune to King William III, who took up residence in Kensington Palace at the end of the 17th century. The Albertopolis complex on the Exhibition Road side was the result of the major cultural influence of Queen Victoria's consort Prince Albert. You will find internationally renowned museums and the Royal Albert Hall, the famously circular concert venue. The nearby pleasant residential area of South Kensington, has been called the 21st *arrondissement* of Paris due to the large numbers of French expats living there. Holland Park to the northwest takes its name from Holland House, an imposing 17th-century country house destroyed during World War II and the area is a haven for wealthy families drawn by the charms of the eponymous park, which boasts a Japanese garden and free-range peacocks. Don't miss the Design Museum, founded by Sir Terence Conran in 1989 and found just round the corner on Kensington High Street.

The King's Road in Chelsea embodied Swinging London at its height, and was a hub for 1960s counterculture figures such as Twiggy, the Rolling Stones, and Mary Quant. Its spirit may have moved on, but the road is still a shopping destination. Knightsbridge, on the southern borders of Hyde Park, is popular with international billionaires drawn to its central location and luxury homes, just around the corner from one of the largest of the royal parks; One Hyde Park is one of the most expensive residential addresses in the world! There is no shortage of luxury boutiques, alongside department store institutions such as Harrods and Harvey Nichols. Belgravia's more discreet elegance is less ostentatious than Mayfair and Knightsbridge. The Grosvenors, a senior aristocratic family, commissioned architect Thomas Cubitt to transform the marshland here into an area of luxury homes at the turn of the 19th century, and Belgravia has since become a haunt of wealthy dynasties and a popular location for embassies; Eaton Square, which is lined with Neoclassical mansions and townhouses, is a perfect example of this architectural refinement.

Last but not least, Notting Hill, once an unassuming suburb, has since become a chic, bohemian enclave of West London, and its colorful Victorian exteriors were immortalized in the movie *Notting Hill* (1999). Thanks to Portobello Road market (which is now very touristic) and a burgeoning artistic community, it became a symbol of alternative culture in the 1980s, but today you will tend to find yoga studios and healthfood cafés in a rather sleepier neighborhood, although the carnival held every summer is a reminder of its multicultural and festive heritage.

HEAVEN AND IN THE EARTH IS THINE THE WIS
KENSINGTON
GORE SW7

THE ESSENTIALS

73

NATURAL HISTORY MUSEUM

This impressive museum, housing more than 80 million items, was designed by architect Alfred Waterhouse during the Victorian era.

74

VICTORIA MEMORIAL

This colossal monument outside Buckingham Palace was sculpted by Thomas Brock in 1911 in honor of Queen Victoria.

75

NOTTING HILL CARNIVAL

The entire area rocks to the rhythm of this street festival to celebrate Caribbean culture, held every last weekend in August since 1966.

76

KENSINGTON PALACE

This historic palace in Kensington Gardens is the official residence of the Prince and Princess of Wales.

77

ROYAL ALBERT HALL

This auditorium built in honor of Prince Albert opened its doors in 1871 and is famous both for its circular shape and its wonderful acoustics.

78

LANCASTER ROAD

The colorful Victorian houses of Lancaster Road are now famous as icons of the Notting Hill area.

79

PORTOBELLO ROAD MARKET

This antiques and vintage market in Notting Hill is the most famous in London, drawing crowds of people with its eclectic atmosphere.

80

KENSINGTON GARDENS

This 274-acre (111-ha) royal park located in Kensington is best known for Kensington Palace, the famous royal residence that was home to Princess Diana.

81

CHELSEA PHYSIC GARDEN

The botanical gardens were founded in 1763 and are a haven of peace and the perfect place for a stroll in the heart of Chelsea.

82

V&A MUSEUM

This museum of British decorative arts has achieved global fame for its program of exhibitions and its rich permanent collection, for which admission is free.

83

DESIGN MUSEUM

Designed by John Pawson, this museum on Kensington High Street houses the finest in design, fashion, architecture, and graphic design.

84

SCIENCE MUSEUM

This Victorian museum on Exhibition Road has been a fount of knowledge for fans of innovation and technology since 1829.

THE DISTILLERY
HOME OF
PORTOBELLO ROAD
№ 171
LONDON DRY GIN
Proud Purveyors
OF
LONDON SPIRIT
PB 1860 RD
VICTUALS & LODGINGS
THE DISTILLERY

ABOVE

It is sometimes tricky to tell the real antiques from tourist reproductions on the stalls of Portobello market.

OPPOSITE

This former 19th-century pub on the Portobello Road is now the headquarters of a local distillery famous for its London dry gin.

ABOVE

It is not uncommon to come across classic cars like this vintage MG in the upmarket area of Chelsea,

OPPOSITE

Cadogan Square in Knightsbridge is known for its Victorian and Queen Anne Revival-style facades, which date from the late 19th century.

HISTORY

PUB CULTURE

Ask any British person what their "local" is and they will definitely have one. With 38,175 licenses issued across the country in 2023, the public house is a pillar of British social life, but it is much more than just a bar.

Nothing stands in the way of a pint at the pub, not even high tide. The White Cross in Richmond issues Wellington boots when the terrace is flooded. The foundations of the pub as an institution were laid by the Romans with their *tabernae* for travelers, and these were followed in turn by medieval alehouses, which were often located in the homes of women who would serve a highly fermented beer (ale) that they had brewed themselves. It was much less risky to drink the ale than the water! It was during this period that the pub really became the focal point of the village, not just for a drink but also to swap news, like a market place. In this spirit, the iconic French House in Soho, a hangout for local intellectuals, still bans cell phones and music.

Urban pubs flourished with the Industrial Revolution and the idea of the "local" established itself, the place across the road where workers would gather at the bar and the middle classes would drink in the saloon. Many of its characteristic architectural features stem from the Victorian era; the Princess Louise in Holborn, with its listed interior, boasts a highly ornate entrance of mosaics and engraved glass, and the extravagant marble and mahogany bar and dark paneling are all original.

The pub has reinvented itself over the years to reflect changing times, with club meetings, union gatherings, family events, darts tournaments, and live gigs. Small pub rock groups started out here in the seventies, famously playing in the relaxed and accessible atmosphere of the Hope and Anchor in Islington and the Tally Ho in Kentish Town (which has since been demolished). Joe Strummer, Dire Straits, and Elvis Costello all made a name for themselves this way.

For the last twenty or so years, pub grub, the typical menu of comfort food has been undergoing something of a facelift, heralding the dawn of gastropubs such as the Marksman in Hackney and The Drapers Arms in Islington. People come here for a pint but also for discerning, regional cuisine, and some establishments have even won Michelin stars! Local craft beers have found their way to the pumps and non-alcoholic options are growing in number with each day that passes, keeping track with developments in British society.

On a winter Sunday, there is nothing to beat a roast dinner with all the trimmings in the pub, a delightful plate of meat and gravy with potatoes, roasted vegetables, and Yorkshire pudding, a kind of baked pancake that is perfect for mopping up the all-important gravy. As soon as the sun returns, head out to the pavement or the tucked-away beer garden to meet up for a pint of lager and a handful of pork scratchings or a Scotch egg.

2

4

1/ THE HOLLY BUSH

This 18th-century pub in a Hampstead lane has exposed beams and a very welcoming atmosphere.

2/ THE DRAPERS ARMS

The extensive wine list, seasonal cooking, and the pub's secret beer garden are just some of the reasons to make your way to Islington.

3/ PRINCESS LOUISE

The rooms behind the listed stained-glass windows of this historic pub in Holborn have been welcoming regulars since Victorian times.

4/ MARKSMAN

This gastropub on Hackney Road in the East End has been carving out a solid reputation for itself on London's culinary scene since being taken over in 2015.

5/ THE WHITE CROSS

This picturesque pub floods at high tide but is a welcome venue for a pint along the Thames at Richmond.

ABOVE

After the bustle of Gloucester Road, the Anglican church of St. Stephen's will immerse you completely in its village atmosphere.

OPPOSITE

The fortunate residents of these Victorian houses in South Kensington have access to a private garden.

ABOVE

Residents in the mews of South Kensington, such as here in Queen's Gate Mews near Hyde Park, have green thumbs.

OPPOSITE

This historic building in South Kensington was built in 1850 and now houses one of the capital's oldest family-run Italian restaurants.

DEEP DIVE

THE ROYAL RESIDENCES

Now home to members of the House of Windsor, the royal residences have been at the heart of power for centuries. While some are scattered across the country, such as the Scottish castle of Balmoral or Sandringham in Norfolk, the majority of these national icons are concentrated in the capital.

There is nothing better than a quick real estate audit to immerse yourself in the history of British royalty. Each of these residences embodies an aspect of tradition and cultural heritage, even if they were intended for different purposes.

Windsor, on the very outskirts of London, is the oldest and largest occupied castle in the world, with opulent Gothic rooms and a round tower. It was strategically constructed on the banks of the Thames by William the Conqueror in the 11th century as a fortified military redoubt and, over the centuries, it has often reprised this role as a place of refuge, in particular during the bombing of London during World War II and the COVID pandemic. St George's Chapel, the last resting place of many a monarch, now hosts the ceremonies of the Order of the Garter, the most senior order of chivalry in the country. Prince Harry and Meghan Markle got married here in 2018.

Buckingham Palace has been the official residence of the British sovereign since the reign of Queen Victoria, and the great and the good of the world troop through this epicenter of public life at banquets and official receptions. It is also where the famous Changing of the Guard takes place. The original version of this most famous of royal residences, built for the Duke of Buckingham in 1703, was rather modest, and it was George IV and his architect John Nash who gave it its current grandiose configuration, with more than 775 rooms. In particular, he was responsible for the iconic balcony from which the royal family greets crowds. The official apartments and gardens are sometimes open to the public.

Just to the southwest of Buckingham Palace you will find a palace that is one of the oldest, but that still plays a key role in the protocol for royal succession. St. James's Palace was built by Henry VIII in the 1530s and was the official residence for three centuries before handing on the torch. This Tudor-style, red-brick building features crenellated walls and turrets, but is not open to the public. The Palladian architecture of Clarence House, next door, is also closed to visitors; it was home to the Queen Mother for a long time, and then to the current king (Charles III) before his coronation, and its royal chapel is still the location for baptisms, marriages, and other family events.

Last but not least, head for leafy Kensington and Chelsea, where King William III, keen to find fresh air far from the great smog of central London, took possession of Kensington Palace in 1689. Nowadays, the palace attracts crowds mainly because of its most famous resident, Princess Diana, who lived here until her death in 1997. Queen Victoria's childhood home is a museum, the headquarters of associations supported by the royal family, and the official London residence of the Prince and Princess of Wales, amongst others.

ROYAL ARCHITECTURE

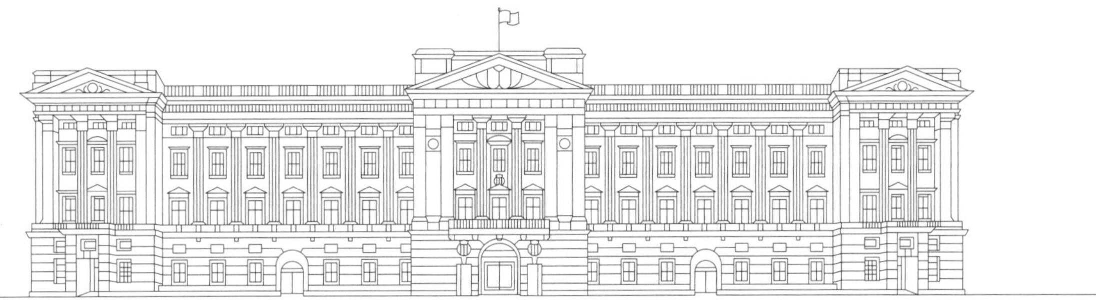

1/ BUCKINGHAM PALACE

The Neoclassical facade of the most famous royal residence in the country is decorated with columns, cornices, and other features inspired by the Ancient World.

2/ KENSINGTON PALACE

The architecture of the palace has evolved over centuries, mixing Baroque and Georgian styles with some Victorian touches.

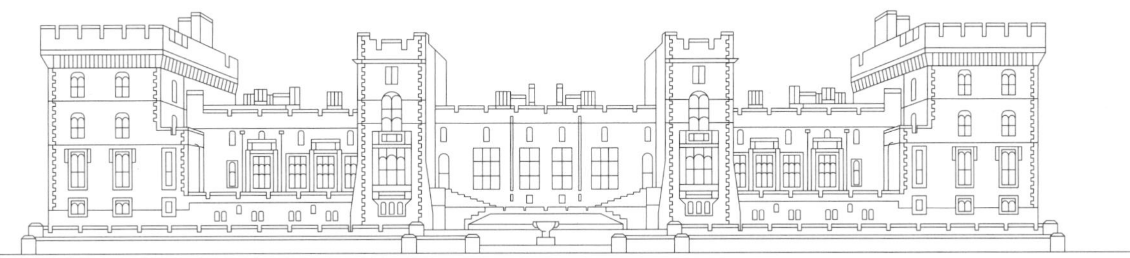

3/ WINDSOR CASTLE

The castle, whose architecture includes features from almost every era since its construction, has kept watch over the Crown for almost ten centuries.

ABOVE

Bennett House in Pimlico's Page Street is part of the Grosvenor Estate, which belongs to the eponymous family.

OPPOSITE

You can enjoy good views of Big Ben and Westminster Palace from the area around Millbank Gardens in Pimlico.

HERRICK
STREET SW1
CITY OF WESTMINSTER
RUSKIN HOUSE

ARCHITECTURE

LONDON BRUTALISM

ROYAL COLLEGE OF PHYSICIANS (RCP)

This Brutalist edifice in Regent's Park opened its doors in 1964. Like many other buildings in the capital, it was the creation of architect Denys Lasdun.

ROWLEY WAY

This housing estate designed by Neave Brown in Camden dates from the 1970s.

CENTREPOINT

This skyscraper on New Oxford Street was designed by George Marsh (R. Seifert and Partners) in the 1960s and has recently been turned into luxury flats.

THE STANDARD LONDON

This hotel opposite St. Pancras was designed by Archer Humphryes and opened its doors in 2019.

TRELLICK TOWER

This tower on the Cheltenham Estate is the work of architect Ernő Goldfinger and has been a Kensal Green icon since 1972.

BARBICAN ESTATE

Don't miss this Brutalist icon. The Barbican complex is also a major cultural institution.

IOE INSTITUTE OF EDUCATION

The proportions of this institute are typical of Brutalist architecture.

ELEPHANT ARCADE

This former parking lot beneath Perronet House has been a shopping mall designed by Turner Works Architects since 2020.

NATIONAL THEATRE

Designed by Denys Lasdun, this building has been home to three theaters since 1976.

Cadogan Square in Knightsbridge is one of the most exclusive squares in the capital.

ART

SAATCHI GALLERY

CONTEMPORARY BOLDNESS

Since its foundation by magnate Charles Saatchi in 1985, the gallery has carved out a unique niche in the landscape of contemporary art. Located just off the King's Road in Chelsea, the Saatchi Gallery is now famous for forty years of daring in the heart of one of London's most fashionable areas.

"The more you love art, the more you get out of it" is a favorite watchword of the Iraqi-British collector born in 1943 and the cofounder of Saatchi & Saatchi advertising agency. Propelled by a desire to make the works of the great names of tomorrow accessible to everyone, he created his own gallery in 1985. "His trademarks? Boldness and courage", explains Amelia Okell, the institution's Head of Communications. The works on show, at the intersection of art and pop culture, are aimed at a broad public and have never shied away from pushing the envelope. Indeed, quite the contrary.

Certain flagship exhibitions will live long in the memory, such as the ones dedicated to the Young British Artists in the 1990s. Damien Hirst's famous shark floating in formalin (*The Physical Impossibility of Death in the Mind of Someone Living*, 1991) is a fixture in the collective visual memory, and Charles Saatchi also shot a number of artists, including Tracey Emin, Marcus Harvey, Cy Twombly and Brice Marden, to the forefront of the scene.

After residencies in St. John's Wood and the Southbank, the gallery migrated to a site just off Sloane Square in 2008. Duke of York Square boasts green spaces, restaurants, boutiques, farmers' markets, and cultural events, and it is here you will find sophisticated local families and knowledgeable tourists strolling on weekends. The thirteen exhibition spaces, redesigned by Allford Hall Monaghan Morris behind the austere Neoclassical exterior, play the minimalist card and let the works speak for themselves. The Saatchi Gallery has put down roots in the neighborhood and keeps pace with the calendar of local events, such as the RHS Chelsea Flower Show, one of the most prestigious horticultural exhibitions in the world, when it gives multidisciplinary artists free reign to bring magic to its gardens.

The gallery was incorporated as a charitable association in 2019 and will support future generations and local communities by continuing its mission to bring art to the masses. While it may no longer exhibit Charles Saatchi's personal collection, its founding principles have not changed. To the surprise and delight of visitors, the works on show are more famous than ever for "artists with varied horizons, disciplines and styles, but who have in common the fact that they are always experimenting", explains Amelia. This is particularly true of *Homelessness: Reframed*, an exhibition recently put on in collaboration with Prince William's Homewards charity. Using works by established artists and talented unknowns of all ages, the Saatchi Gallery brought the story of the country's homeless into the museum, restoring their dignity while also continuing to break down the barriers of the genre.

AMELIA OKELL

Head of Communications Amelia Okell stands amid the works on the first floor of the gallery.

A LEAFY OASIS

The site on Duke of York Square is the perfect place for a stroll after visiting the gallery.

ABOVE

The Art Deco decor of the Regency Cafe with its wall tiles is typical of London cafés from the 1940s. The establishment is now a listed building.

OPPOSITE

The atmosphere and traditional British cooking of this greasy spoon (see p. 234) make it a real London classic.

REGENCY
STREET SW1
CITY OF WESTMINSTER
REGENCY CAFE
EXIT ONLY

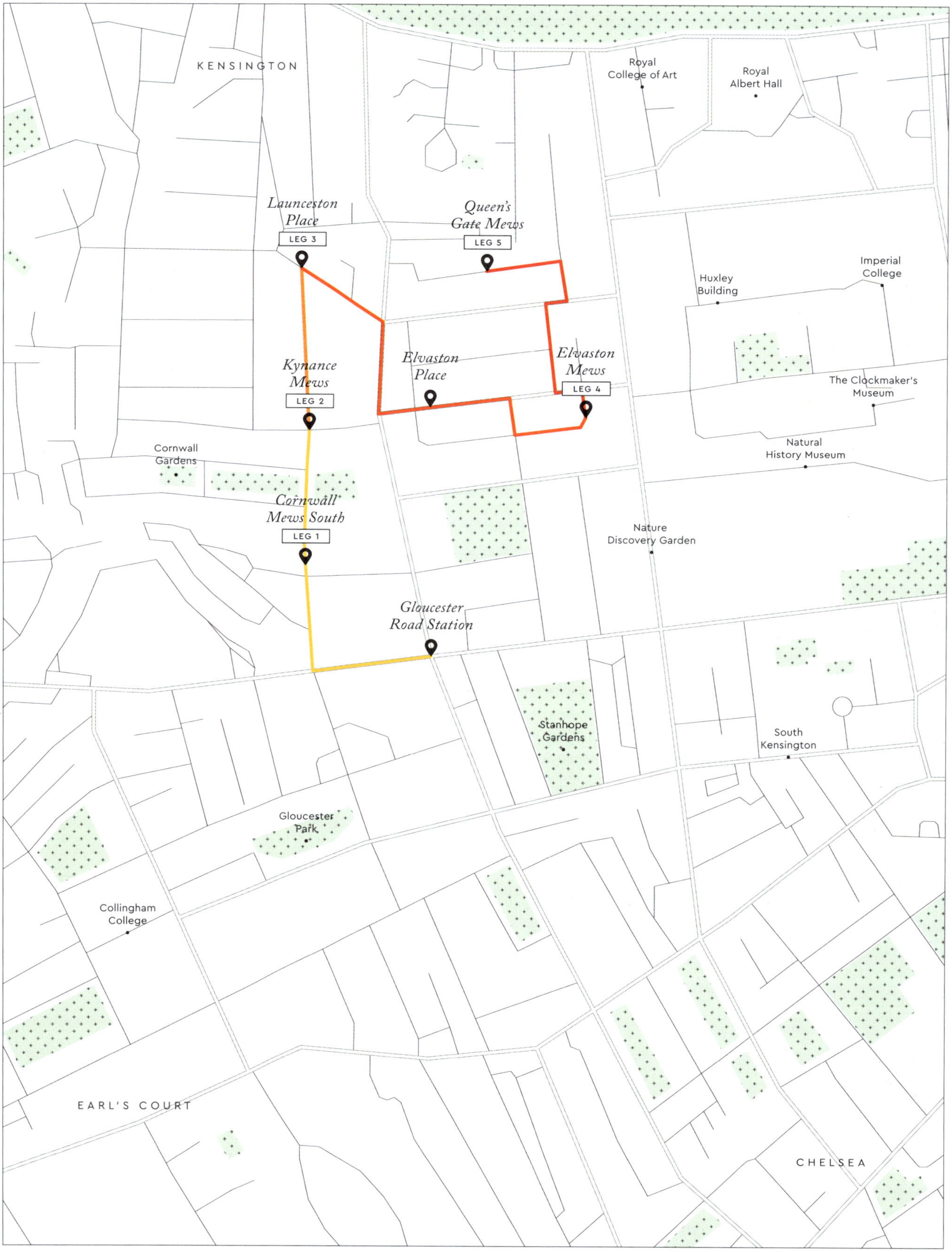

KENSINGTON

Royal College of Art

Royal Albert Hall

Launceston Place
LEG 3

Queen's Gate Mews
LEG 5

Huxley Building

Imperial College

Kynance Mews
LEG 2

Elvaston Place

Elvaston Mews
LEG 4

The Clockmaker's Museum

Cornwall Gardens

Natural History Museum

Cornwall Mews South
LEG 1

Nature Discovery Garden

Gloucester Road Station

Stanhope Gardens

South Kensington

Gloucester Park

Collingham College

EARL'S COURT

CHELSEA

THE MEWS OF SOUTH KENSINGTON

As you stroll around the streets of South Kensington, you may easily find yourself turning into one of these unassuming cobbled alleyways. Once the stables, carriage houses, and servants' quarters for the imposing townhouses of the 17th to 19th centuries, the mews have been reinvented as homes much sought-after for the luxury of their discreet charm.

LEG 1 : CORNWALL MEWS SOUTH

Take a left out of the green-tiled exit of Gloucester Road station and turn left onto the Cromwell Road before taking a right up Grenville Place. Divided into two halves, the urban jungle of Cornwall Mews gradually narrows as you advance along its western arm, reaching a particularly bucolic section with hortensias, lilacs, and arches of jasmine at number 12. On the east side, the exterior of number 7 seems to be from another era, with scalloped lead flashing and a red-brick bay window. An astonishing peace reigns in the mews, in the very heart of the city.

LEG 2 : KYNANCE MEWS

Cross Cornwall Gardens to the north and proceed to Kynance Mews on Launceston Place, without doubt one of the most photogenic mews of its kind (discretion is advised to respect the privacy of the residents). Built in the 1860s, it checks every box the imagination might link to these Victorian alleys, with pastel facades, old cottages, ornate ironwork, and even a hint of classical music from a window! Come the fall, photos of the arch at the entrance, draped in Virgina creepers, are all over social media. Take a moment to explore the kitchen garden of neighboring Christ Church Kensington, just around the corner.

LEG 3 : LAUNCESTON PLACE

Between the two mews, head along charming Launceston Place to the eponymous square at its northern end; with its patisserie, florists, gourmet restaurant, and art gallery, it has all the sophisticated tranquility that is typical of South Kensington.

LEG 4 : ELVASTON MEWS

Proceed to Elvaston Place, and then Elvaston Mews, just a couple of minutes away. Built in the 1830s, it is a fine example of the architecture typical of these little alleys, with stables on the first floor and servants' quarters above, and large doors to admit carriages. On the corner there is a pretty almond-green exterior festooned with wisteria. Legend has it that the stable at number 11 retained its original function into the 2000s. Finally, admire the wrought-iron gallery of the imposing red-brick building with the white moldings that stands proudly at the end of the mews.

LEG 5 : QUEEN'S GATE MEWS

Queen's Gate Mews, our final stop, is one of the largest in the area and is also one of the few to have a pub. The traditional decor of the Queen's Arms is a welcome stop for refreshment before an exploration of Hyde Park.

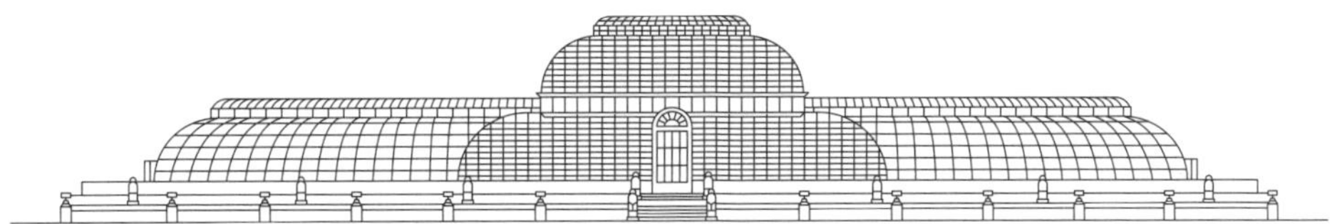

GREENWICH, HACKNEY, HIGHGATE, RICHMOND UPON THAMES, STRATFORD

GREATER LONDON

It is impossible to restrict the metropolis to its central area (zones 1 and 2) and even more impossible to try to sum up the immense diversity of this sprawling city spread over six zones and 607 square miles (1,572 km^2). From the vast expanses of greenery in Richmond to the urban redevelopment of Stratford, London is a city of a thousand faces.

P.224

The view right across the City from the hill of the Royal Observatory in Greenwich.

OPPOSITE

Several small boutiques with typical London exteriors line Highgate High Street.

The rural, village-like towns on the banks of the Thames to the southwest, like the borough of Richmond upon Thames, are popular with wealthy families looking for some peace and quiet, a green setting, and famous schools. Richmond upon Thames is known for its park, replete with deer that roam free, and the famous royal botanical gardens at Kew. The panorama of the Thames valley from Richmond Hill has inspired artists like the painter William Turner (1778-1851), and it is difficult to imagine that you are still in the city! The tranquil residential area of Wimbledon, just around the corner, hosts the world's oldest tennis championship every summer and lastly, the historic icon of Hampton Court Palace leads on to the royal borough of Kingston upon Thames, much beloved of rowing fans. The Coronation Stone, where Saxon kings of the 10th century were crowned, is on display in the center of Kingston.

The borough of Greenwich to the southeast, on the opposite bank to the Isle of Dogs, boasts a proud scientific, maritime, and architectural heritage. The Royal Observatory, Greenwich, the site of the Prime Meridian, is located on a hill in the eponymous royal park, with stunning views over Canary Wharf and the Thames. Nearer the riverbank, the *Cutty Sark*, a famous clipper, still bears witness to the former might of British maritime trade, and the prominent architect Christopher Wren (1632-1723) designed the principal buildings, including the Observatory and the British Baroque-style Old Royal Naval College. The complex has been declared by UNESCO as a World Heritage Site.

Highgate Village on the edge of the parkland of Hampstead Heath in the northwest has always attracted artists and literary figures, including the poet John Keats. The living is easy in this green and tranquil area, and its famous cemetery is a Gothic masterpiece.

Hackney Wick to the east is a paradise of microbreweries, artists' workshops, and street art, while the vast expanses of Hackney Marshes, crossed by the River Lea to the north, are the perfect spot for a peaceful stroll.

Lastly, there is always something new in the northeast, especially in the boroughs of Waltham Forest and Haringey. Leyton, for example, was recently voted one of the coolest areas in the world by *Time Out* magazine and is on the up and up. Due to its proximity to Stratford, the area was spruced up for the 2012 Olympic Games and its location to the north of Hackney is attracting creative communities forced out by rising rents. The circumference of the city continues to expand.

55A
VILLAGE FLOWERS
HIGHGATE · N6
020 8347 0721
FLORIST
55B

THE ESSENTIALS

85

MARITIME GREENWICH

This collection of buildings in southeast London are testimony to British artistic and scientific endeavors during the 17th and 18th centuries.

86

RICHMOND PARK

This 3½-square mile (9.5-km^2) royal park in the southwest of the capital is the jewel in the crown of the wealthy area of Richmond upon Thames.

87

CANARY WHARF

This business district is spread out over about 100 acres (40 ha) along the Thames.

88

HACKNEY WICK

Artists' workshops and creative projects have breathed new life into the formerly industrial area of Hackney Wick beside the Lea.

89

STRATFORD

Stratford in the East End of London has enjoyed a new lease of life after its reinvigoration for the 2012 Olympics.

90

HIGHGATE VILLAGE

The leafy slopes of Highgate in northwest London have a distinctly rural British feel.

91

KEW GARDENS

The 300 acres (121 ha) of these royal botanical gardens to the southwest of Greater London are a world in themselves.

Once a dockyard, Limehouse Basin, which links the Thames to the canals of London, is now a marina and a perfect spot for a relaxing stroll.

Together

ABOVE

The typical Neoclassical colonnades on either side of the Queen's House were added in the 19th century.

OPPOSITE

Some of the buildings of the Old Royal Naval College in Greenwich, which was designed by Christopher Wren and was once the training college for Royal Navy officers, are open to the public.

FOOD AND DRINK

NORMAN'S

GREASY SPOON 2.0

Elliott Kaye and Richie Hayes have been stylishly redefining the parameters of the greasy spoon in Tufnell Park since 2020. Catch a glimpse of all things retro with this resolutely new old-school café as we take a nostalgic dive into the classics of British cooking.

Norman's seems to have always been there, tucked away behind its red gingham drapes, a quiet café in an unassuming corner of north Islington, just round the corner from Archway Tube station. But this paean to the fry-up, the classic British breakfast, by chefs Elliott Kaye and Richie Hayes, emerged only in 2020 to "celebrate the very essence of the greasy spoon," as Elliott explains.

These no-frills cafés first appeared at the beginning of the Industrial Revolution, serving solid but affordable food that was often fatty (hence the name) to the nascent working classes of the late 19th century. By the 1950s, the greasy spoon had spread and become a cherished British icon. With basic but welcoming decor, and unpretentious cooking that delivers no surprises, its very familiarity is its charm, especially as many have been driven out by soulless chains in recent years. These local cafés see all walks of life meeting up for a full English or a cup of builder's tea, the black brew with milk and sugar that construction workers knock back by the pint. These venues are known both colloquially and affectionately as the "caff".

Since their first encounter in a kitchen ten years ago, these two young chefs with impeccable resumes "have always known that they would open their own caff one day", Elliott informs us, and the deed was finally done in 2020. The two partners have left no detail to chance: Formica tables, red gingham drapes, checkered lino flooring; their retro vision, mixed with minimalism, is right on the mark. Named in honor of Richie's great-grandfather, Norman's is intended to be "welcoming and open to all". Nostalgia is in play, and "a mixture of workers, pensioners, musicians, stylists, filmmakers, and even restaurateurs pop in," recounts Elliott.

On the plate, the pair revisit the classic repertoire of the genre, reinterpreted with carefully selected ingredients. The sausages in the full English are farm-sourced, the brown sauce is made in-house, the filter coffee is a specialty, and the beans homemade. For lunch, try the Welsh rarebit (toast with melted Welsh cheese) or the classic ham, egg, and chips, with its generous plate of thick-cut fries and a slice of roasted ham, topped with a fried egg. The menu and the atmosphere changes in the evening as they explore their creativity with "a version of Norman's by night," emphasizes Richie. This brilliantly executed division of powers explains why a restaurant paying its dues has become a destination of choice on the London culinary scene, buoyed up by crazy success on social networks. Pop-ups with chef friends, regular product drops, collaborations with national institutions such as Burberry – their reach extends well beyond that of simple local café. Norman's is just getting started.

1/ A UNIQUE CAFE

Nestling between an upholsterer's and a liquor store, Norman's punchy sign stands out on Junction Road, setting the tone.

2/ A DUO ON THE RISE

These two fashionable chefs have always dreamed of having their own place.

3/ ENGLISH BREAKFAST AND PLAYING BY THE RULES

British classics rub shoulders with a cup of builder's tea (served with milk, as is only right) on the breakfast table.

4/ À LA CARTE

The ingredients of the iconic full English have an impeccable pedigree in the British café.

5/ THE AESTHETICS

From the furniture to the photos of the England football team, the tiny café has been meticulously designed down to the smallest detail.

ABOVE

The dome of the famous Observatory at Greenwich houses the Great Equatorial Telescope.

OPPOSITE

The Greenwich Prime Meridian is the international benchmark of longitude and passes through the astronomical observatory, which overlooks the park.

ARTS AND CRAFTS

FLORIAN GADSBY

ANGLO-JAPANESE CERAMICS

Leading the field of a new generation of urban artisans, ceramicist Florian Gadsby has amassed millions of subscribers as he cultivates his taste for functional pieces of stoneware of carefully studied simplicity. We met this discreet perfectionist in his High Barnet studio.

His workshop, a former dry cleaner's, is located at the end of a small road in this quiet, leafy suburb at the end of the Northern Line in northern Greater London, and the surrounding, formerly industrial, buildings are home to an Italian rock group, a photo studio, and even an opera singer. With its exposed beams and painted bricks, the space is bathed in light but also particularly tidy, like the ceramicist himself. A photogenic drying rack, a hangover from the place's previous existence, hangs from the ceiling. At our feet sits Miso, Florian's shiba inu, a constant companion during his daily tasks.

Florian Gadsby was introduced to pottery at a very early age at his Ruldolf Steiner school. It was not initially love at first sight, but "a desire to persevere, as [I was] finally good at something!" he says with a smile. After a work placement at the renowned Leach Pottery school/workshop in St. Ives in Cornwall, he headed to Ireland and then to the workshop of potter Lisa Hammond (Maze Hill Pottery) in Greenwich, where he refined his skills as an apprentice. After returning from six months spent in Japan with renowned master potter Ken Matsuzaki, he launched his first online sale in 2017, achieving immediate success. Since then, more than 15,000 people scramble for each of his drops, and the quickest off the mark manage to snag a bowl or a mug with austere lines and sharp angles, along which enamels fired in a reduction atmosphere have left a unique furrow. A parallel market has sprung up on eBay, with prices skyrocketing, because this experienced ceramicist is also a social media star, with millions of people following his behind-the-scenes activities and educational content on a daily basis.

Florian is a contemporary figure following in the footsteps of a mid-20th-century movement of pottery studios that advocated a return to traditional craft values. Spurred on by now-famous figures such as Bernard Leach, Lucie Rie, and Hans Coper, these committed artisans sought a response to industrialization in the creation of functional but unique pieces that blurred the boundaries between arts and crafts. "Thanks to social networks, I now feel part of a vast international community of urban artisans", he explains.

A creator of art whose time has now come, the discreet Florian likes to leave things open to interpretation. His Japanese/British-influenced fine pieces are utilitarian but "are also displayed like sculptures", as his studio shelves reveal, on which he arranges paintings according to the shape and height of each object. His aim is to "create shapes that are so easy to identify [that he can] explore the realm of possibilities for clay and enamel." Mission accomplished.

DEMANDING

Florian Gadsby's pieces reflect with rare precision the ceramicist's quest for excellence.

BEAUTIFULLY STAGED

Pieces just out of the kiln line up with finished works on the shelves to create a carefully curated harmony.

ABOVE

Leafy paths full of bucolic charm offer tempting strolls in the center of Richmond village.

OPPOSITE

Cholmondeley Walk follows the Thames at Richmond, taking you past boathouses and swanky houses.

ABOVE

It's easy to see how Duck's Walk in Richmond got its name.

OPPOSITE

Between March and October, you can hire a boat just by Richmond Bridge and take a restful trip on the Thames.

DEEP DIVE

LONDON'S PUBLIC TRANSPORT

"The world's mine oyster", as William Shakespeare pointed out in *The Merry Wives of Windsor* in 1602, and the Oyster Card neatly unlocks the sprawling public transit network of Transport for London (TfL). It is definitely the best way to explore the many nooks and crannies of the vast capital.

The London Underground opened in 1863 as the world's first underground railway, with the very first line connecting Paddington to Farringdon. It was nicknamed the "Tube" in reference to the cylindrical shape of its tunnels, and some of its stations have been dug out deep in the bowels of the city. This is certainly the case at Hampstead, whose users plunge to a depth of 192 feet (58.5 m) below ground! With 250 miles (402 km) of track spread across eleven lines, the Tube is one of the biggest networks in existence and is easy to identify by its iconic red and blue logo. The Elizabeth Line was the most recent route to open in 2022.

If you want to go up in the world, nothing beats a trip on board one of the famous red double-decker buses, iconic symbols of the city that were introduced in 1910. With more than 9,000 vehicles, 700 routes that run all day and night, and fares that are more affordable than the Tube, they are also the transport mode of choice for many Londoners. Crossing the Thames while sitting in the front row of the top deck is a panoramic tourist adventure in itself.

Cyclists are also an essential part of the urban landscape. You only need take a look at the rush-hour traffic on the seven cycle superhighways dedicated to them, come rain or shine! Development of the superhighways took a major turn in 2010, when TfL introduced access to bicycles known as Boris bikes in a nod to Boris Johnson, then the Mayor of London, and the nickname has passed into common usage. The number of cyclists skyrocketed after the pandemic, prompting Mayor Sadiq Khan to announce that "cycling [is] an integral part of our vision of a more livable city". The network has undergone constant improvement since then, with the development of new infrastructure like protected cycle tracks, parking spots reserved for cycles, and low-speed zones.

In some boroughs in the east and south with little or no access to the Tube, it is often easier to get about on two wheels. To improve accessibility in these areas, the Ginger Line (East London Line) and the DLR (Docklands Light Railway) have been extended to complement the bus network, and these light trains play a key role in residents' mobility.

Although journeys by public transport can sometimes seem endless because of the sheer size of the city, they are often more efficient that taking a black cab. You should still enjoy a ride in one of these iconic taxis some time, and start a conversation with the cabbie. These taxi drivers know the city like the back of their hands.

LONDON UNDERGROUND

1/ THE DEEPEST STATION ON THE LONDON UNDERGROUND

With a depth of 192 feet (58.5 m), Hampstead station on the Northern Line is the deepest on the network. The escalator leading to the platforms has 320 steps!

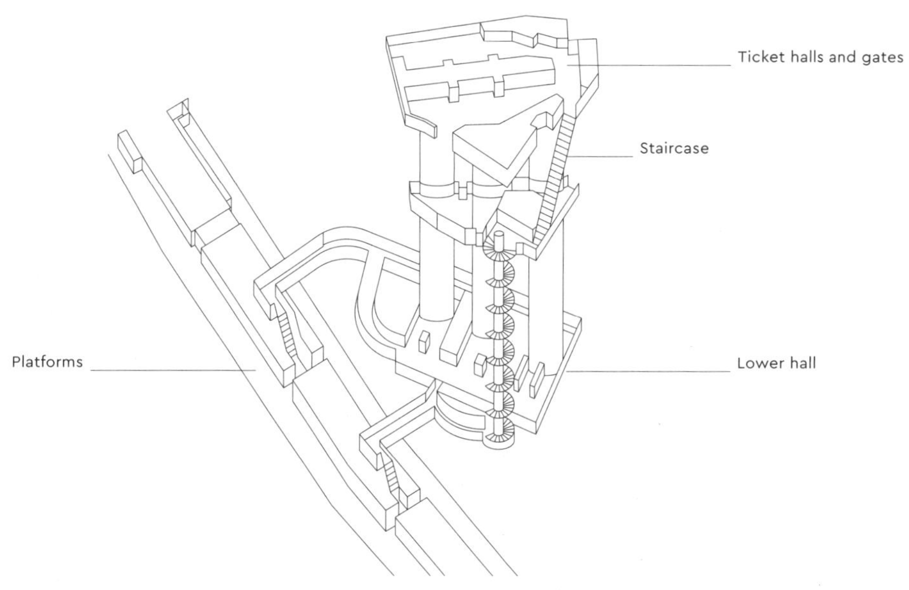

2/ THE EVOLUTION OF CARRIAGE DESIGN

From the first wooden carriages of 1863 to today's automated trains, Tube design has changed over time. Some older specimens are on display in the Transport Museum in Covent Garden.

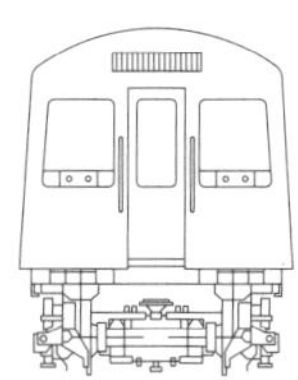

D78 STOCK

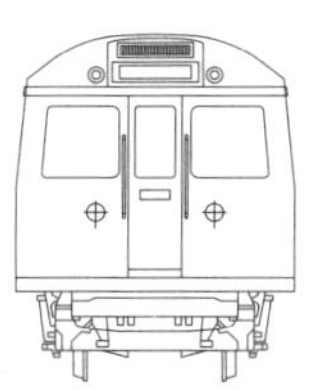

C69 AND C77 STOCK

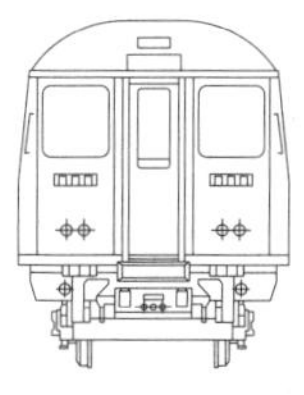

A60 AND A62 STOCK

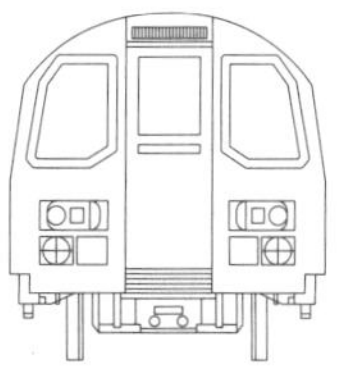

1995 STOCK

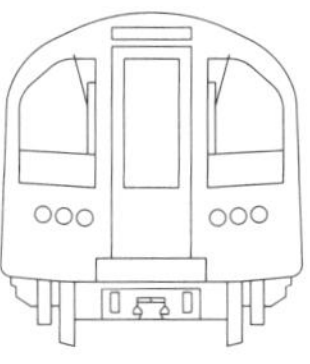

1992 STOCK

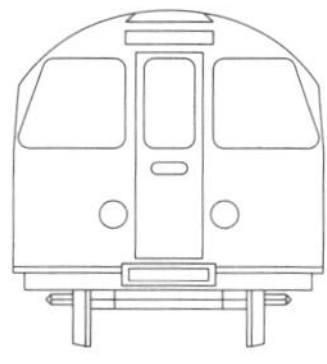

1967 TUBE STOCK

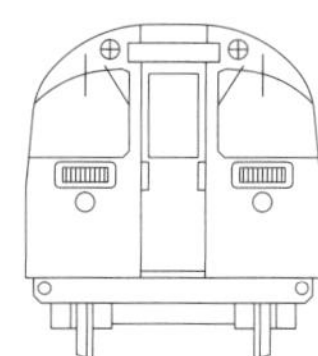

1973 STOCK

ABOVE

Petersham Nurseries was once a tree nursery but is now a classic destination for lovers of plants and antiques.

OPPOSITE

A mixture of vintage furniture, Italian gourmet food, and terracotta pots has made Richmond's Petersham Nurseries a success.

NATURE

KEW GARDENS

THE BOTANICAL BRASSERIE

Visitors to the original museum (built in 1857) can enjoy lunch or afternoon tea with breathtaking views across the pond to the Palm House.

PRINCESS OF WALES CONSERVATORY

This 1980s greenhouse named after Princess Diana celebrates ecosystems from all over the world.

BIRD'S-EYE VIEW

The best observation point in the Palm House is of course the balcony, perched some 30 feet (10 m) above the trees.

PALM HOUSE

Built in 1848, this greenhouse is home to the botanical garden's tropical species.

TEMPERATE HOUSE

This Victorian greenhouse is a paradise for species from temperate climates.

MID-SEASON FORM

The charms of *Victoria boliviana* are on full display in the Waterlily House during the summer, a must-see little gem.

WATERLILY HOUSE

Climbing plants are gradually taking over the glazed roof of the greenhouse.

PRINCESS OF WALES CONSERVATORY

Cacti rub shoulders with other plants from all four corners of the world in this global greenhouse.

WATERLILY HOUSE

This magnificent small square greenhouse famous for its giant waterlilies is a haven for all aquatic plants.

ABOVE

Ferns abound in the wetlands of Richmond Park, which is also famed for its thousands of centuries-old trees.

OPPOSITE

The deer in Richmond Park shape its 2,360 acres (955 ha) of grassland as they graze.

ABOVE

Pen Ponds is the best known of Richmond Park's twenty-five watercourses and regularly attracts terns, gulls, and other seabirds.

OPPOSITE

The 2,360 acres (955 ha) of Richmond Park, the capital's largest royal park, are crisscrossed with paths.

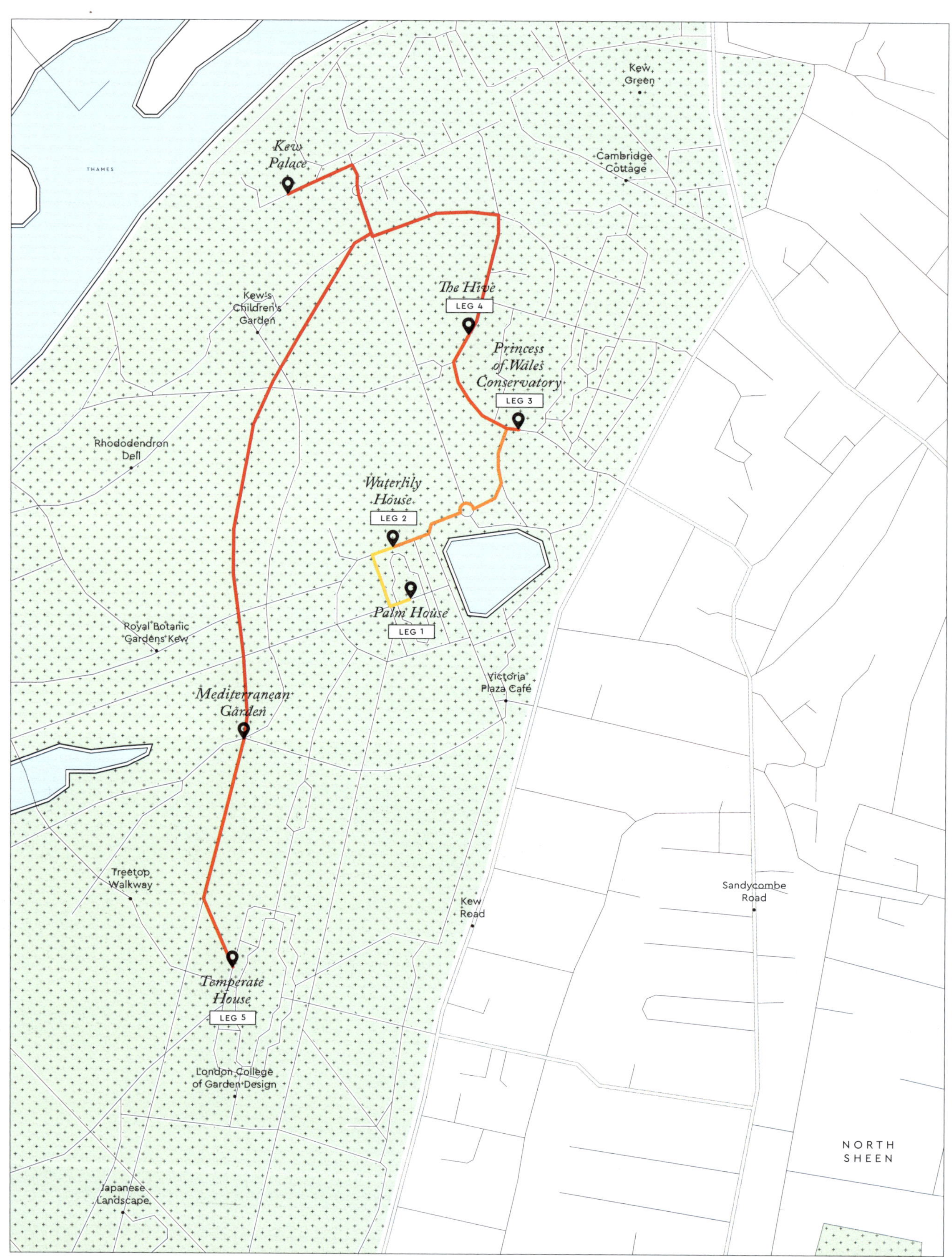
Kew Green
THAMES
Kew Palace
Cambridge Cottage
The Hive
LEG 4
Kew's Children's Garden
Princess of Wales Conservatory
LEG 3
Rhododendron Dell
Waterlily House
LEG 2
Palm House
LEG 1
Royal Botanic Gardens Kew
Victoria Plaza Café
Mediterranean Garden
Treetop Walkway
Kew Road
Sandycombe Road
Temperate House
LEG 5
London College of Garden Design
NORTH SHEEN
Japanese Landscape

WALKING TOUR

KEW GARDENS

Kew Gardens in southwest London were founded in 1759 and have now been declared a UNESCO World Heritage Site. This 326-acre (132-hectare) park is one of the best-stocked botanical gardens in the world and home to some 50,000 trees and plants from around the globe. Londoners love to escape here for a stroll in its green landscape, just a few stops along the District Line or Overground.

LEG 1 : PALM HOUSE

Enter via the Victoria Gate entrance and dive straight into the heart of nature. The first stop is the legendary Palm House, a superb Victorian greenhouse; the tropical atmosphere within its glass and metal structure never fails to astonish, with a temperature of 95°F (35°C) and 80 percent humidity (and sometimes more). It is a paradise for exotic plants like banana trees, ferns, and carnivorous plants. Some of the palm trees can grow to a height of 52 feet (16 m)! Climb the spiral staircase for a bird's-eye view across the tropical canopy from the balcony perched more than 30 feet (10 m) above ground, as rays of sunlight filter through the palm fronds.

LEG 2 : WATERLILY HOUSE

Getting back to more British temperatures, the Victorian Waterlily House provides a radical change of atmosphere. It is dedicated to aquatic plants and has become famous for its giant waterlilies, some of which can grow to 5 feet (1.5 m) in diameter! Watch how the flowers unfold in the sunlight during summer.

LEG 3 : THE PRINCESS OF WALES CONSERVATORY

Follow the path leading to this more modern greenhouse opened by Princess Diana in 1987. Each of its sections is laid out as a labyrinth and celebrates a separate ecosystem. You will find a wide variety of climates and species from all over the world, from arid desert cacti to luxuriant cloud forest plants. Continue your exploration with a trip to the kitchen garden and Alpine rock garden at the back.

LEG 4 : THE HIVE AND KEW PALACE

Return to the main path and *The Hive* will soon appear. This 56-ft (17-m) art installation by the architect and designer Wolfgang Buttress raises public awareness of the essential role played by bees in our ecosystem. Construction of the structure, which opened in 2016 as a tribute to beehives, required 170,000 pieces of aluminum. Now stroll on to Kew Palace, the former summer residence of King George III, and admire its brick facade, built in the 18th century.

LEG 5 : TEMPERATE HOUSE

Our last stop is the majestic Temperate House, standing in absolute tranquility at the end of the long and leafy path of Love Lane. You might even spot outdoor drawing classes in progress as you stroll. The largest Victorian greenhouse in the world is 164 feet (50 m) long and 53 feet (16 m) high, and was completely renovated in 2018. With giant sequoia, tree ferns, acacia, bamboo, and cycads, there are some 1,500 temperate species living in harmony here.

BIOGRAPHY

Journalist and ceramicist **Valentine Benoist** has been roaming London for nearly fifteen years in search of all that is good and beautiful in her adopted city, and she now divides her time between the UK capital and Brittany. This book shines a spotlight on a particular way of life in London, nourished by inspiring encounters off the beaten track.

myhungryvalentine.com / @myhungryvalentine

Acknowledgments: thanks are due to Chach, Cecil, and Camille, my favorite Londoners, and to Ale and Charlie for their unwavering support. Thank you to Laura for her photos which have spiced up this new joint project and to Faris for giving us the opportunity to tell the story of our London together.

Food and lifestyle photographer **Laura Jalbert** lives and works in London and Sète. Originally from Nîmes, love brought her to the UK capital in 2018, and she ended up falling in love with the city. She uses her images to highlight the beautiful work of hard-working people sharing the same values of producing sustainable, handmade, natural food and drinks.

jajafoodstudio.com / Instagram @jajafoodstudio

Acknowledgments: thank you to Hugo for having shown me London and much more, to my parents Dominique and Jean for their unconditional support, to Valentine, my multitalented partner and friend, and to Faris, to Sabine, and to the Chêne team from this second beautiful project.

PHOTOGRAPHIC CREDITS

All the photographs in this book are by Laura Jalbert, with the exception of: © Barbara Muller/Alamy image bank: 119; © Better.org: 95; © Charlie Harris/Unsplash: 189; © House of Hackney: 181; © Jack Hobhouse/Alamy image bank: 119; © The Ned, Morris: 22-23; © Tj Holowaychuk/Unsplash: 189; © The City of London Corporation: 95; © UrbanImages/Alamy image bank: 118; © Young Jeffrey/Unsplash: 189.

First published in English in 2025
by Rizzoli Universe, a division of
Rizzoli International Publications

Rizzoli International Publications Inc
49 West 27th Street
New York, NY 10001

Rizzoli International Publications UK Ltd
Somerset House, West Wing
Strand, London WC2R 1LA

www.rizzoliusa.com

Originally published in French in 2025 as
Petit Atlas Hédoniste – London
by © 2025, Éditions du Chêne – Hachette Livre
www.editionsduchene.fr

For Rizzoli
Publisher: Charles Miers
Associate Publisher: Tina Persaud
Senior Editor: Kristy Richardson

For Éditions du Chêne
Editor-in chief: Emmanuel Le Vallois
Artistic director: Sabine Houplain

ISBN 978-0-7893-4434-2

2025 / 1
Printed in China

The authorized representative in the EU for safety and compliance is Mondadori Libri S.p.A., via Gian Battista Vico 42, Milan, Italy, 0123, www.mondadori.it

Visit us online: Instagram.com/RizzoliBooks
Facebook.com/RizzoliNewYork
Youtube.com/user/RizzoliNY